SNIPPETS

OF A

GRANDFATHER'S LIFE

Ron Thompson

Published by Masterful Life-Performance Press
576 Lightening Ridge Road
Plainfield, Vermont 05667
www.masterfullifeperformance.com

ISBN Number 979-8-3305-9517-4

CONTENTS

INTENT

To Ashley, Aaron, Kai and Kent,

    The intent of this little book is to entertain you and pass on a legacy of my personal values. I trust you will notice that seeking a love-based solution to challenge is my most strongly held value. The foundation for this personal value is simple:

Love Is.

Please agree with me that, always and everywhere, Love Is.

Ron Thompson, Your Grandfather

A guiding principle in my mom's life was "Life is too short to be unhappy." She had a relatively short, but very happy life, living only 53 years (1912-1965). Her marriage to my dad was a primary source of joy, he her loyal, adoring and talent-laden life partner. Her happiness was augmented by her love for her two sons (Richard and Ronald), dozens of good friends, and a relaxed 1950's California homemaker lifestyle.

Mom was a curvy, blond, girl-next-door beauty, five feet tall (in high heels). Perky but not overstated. You wouldn't think of being uncomfortable around her. She was at ease. In her presence it was about you. A natural non-invasive curiosity, sprinkled with perception and optimism.

I recall her mentioning her fondness for Greek and Roman mythology and her being proud of writing a paper on the indigenous tribes of the Sacramento-San Joaquin Valley while attending College of the Pacific.

She kept her fingernails painted deep Revlon red, and often sunbathed in our backyard in her two-piece sunsuit, dousing her hair with lemon juice from our Meyer lemon tree, listening to the Yankees-Dodgers games on the transistor radio. Having a rich tan and being truly blond was important to her.

And those fingernails came in handy.

One weekday, after coming home from kindergarten, I went with Mom across the street to neighbor Irene's house for lunch. It was a typical 1940's lunch, hotdogs, potato salad, Coke and potato chips. We sat around

Irene's kitchen breakfast nook eating. I began gagging with a facial expression that let everybody know, without a doubt, I was on my way out. With no hesitation Mom was on me. One of those Revlon red fingernails went right down my throat, hooked that stuck piece of hotdog and ripped it out of my windpipe. I don't remember what came next. I suppose I finished my lunch…in small bites.

Tootie saved my life.

Evelyn "Tootie" Thompson

Nancy was my first friend. I lived at 240 40th Street and she at 255 40th Street. Her little house was across the street from my little house, in the sun-drenched 1940's Sacramento, California neighborhood.

We first met when I was four and she was five. She went to school first. I was surprised and indignant. What do you mean, girls going to school first? Boys should be first. Yes, masculine privilege in the raw.

At ages nine and eight (please note that I put Nancy's age first), we played Monopoly in her bedroom. Well, it wasn't quite the Monopoly as advertised. It was more like Doctor Monopoly. The primary rule was something like this: If you passed GO, you got to do a doctor visit with the other player. I learned a lot from Nancy, and she from me.

Among the other lessons, I learned the meaning of disappointment.

Somewhere in our pre-teen years Nancy had a conversation with her mother, Irene. Nancy stopped wanting to play Monopoly.

It's been over seven decades since our last game, and obviously I have not gotten over the rejection. It's like wanting to land on Boardwalk and drawing the Go To Jail card instead.

Go To Jail Card

The prefrontal cortex of the human brain is the seat of empathic forethought and judgment. It is pretty much fully developed by age twenty-five. At age ten, mine was in the embryonic stage of black-and-white moralistic thinking, devoid of empathic forethought.

Billy was my next-door playmate. It's not that I particularly liked playing with Billy (he found a way to cheat, even at Monopoly) but often he was the only boy my age readily available on my block.

And it wasn't just the fact that he compulsively cheated. When I went to his mother, Alice, to report his behavior, she backed him up.

That infuriated me once too often. I exploded with tears of frustration when I told my mother about the injustice. Later, when I was less emotional, I plotted my retribution.

On the inner wall of my and my brother's bedroom closet was a metallic box-like insert, held between the wall studs by two screws, and used for vertical shoe storage. When the screws were carefully removed, and the metal insert taken out, a roomy hiding place became revealed. Over the years my brother and I kept some interesting things in there, stuff to which my parents were certainly not privy.

At age ten my stuff consisted primarily of my fireworks collection, purchased with my allowance from under-the-counter sources during visits to San Francisco's Chinatown. During later years, one could find calendars (use your imagination), and even later, condoms (wrapped entirely with great expectations).

My retribution plan included fireworks. I removed two firecrackers, one Medium-sized and one larger Red Devil from the cache. Without telling him anything, casually I asked my brother which firecracker was the LEAST powerful. In typical big-brother fashion, he pointed to the Red Devil.

So, I took the Red Devil and a book of matches next door. When Billy came out to play with me in his front yard, I asked him to play a new game. It was called Queeny, and to play it, he had to close his eyes and turn around, which he did. Very deliberately and swiftly the Red Devil was lit and slipped into his back left jeans pocket.

The rest is history, burned into my memory, into the panic-faced Alice as she ripped Billy's jeans down, and into the three-inch powder burn on Billy's left cheek.

I immediately ran home and gave my entire fireworks collection to my brother, a move I later deeply regretted.

Nothing was said to me by either set of parents; however, I never played with Billy again.

Now, as a psychologist, I cringe at the thought of my early eye-for-eye, tooth-for-tooth ethical behavior, and for the damage to Billy, perpetrated in the name of self-righteous justice.

And from time to time, the thought crosses my mind that when I die, I'm going to go straight to Hell. Thank goodness I have my study of developmental psychology and neuroscience to quiet my guilt.

My paternal grandmother, Elizabeth Monahan Thompson (Lizzie), was seventy-seven years old in 1942, the year of my birth. She was born in 1865 (Moville, County Donegal, Ireland). Elizabeth was one of nine children born to William Beatty Monahan, a tenant farmer and Methodist minister, and Mary Hepworth Monahan.

Elizabeth was a woman whose demeanor and opinions reflected insights born of a life in which all challenges were met with intellectual brilliance. And she did enjoy intellectual brilliance.

She was a life-long learner, holding a Life Teaching Certificate from Queens College, Yorkshire, England, a California State Teachers Certificate from San Jose State College, and doing post-graduate studies at Cal. Berkeley. She was a skilled soprano and pianist. She was fluent in Greek, Hebrew, Russian, Italian, Spanish, French, and German. During WWII she translated German documents for the United States Government. At age seventy-five she walked up the hill from her modest stucco house on Cherry Street to Cal. Berkeley for her classes in Russian. Her linguistic swansong was to read War and Peace in Russian.

During several periods in her life she taught for a living. Late in life she was a teacher of developmentally disabled children. Handwritten on the back of an old photo is the inscription: "Elizabeth Thompson and her class of dimwits." In that photo Grandmother's face glows with a warm smile.

I recall two things about her kitchen. The first is that there was always a book (not a cookbook) propped up on the sink next to the gas stove. The second was the odor of burnt steak. Information was Grandmother's real food.

A mildly problematic traveling partner to her intellectual brilliance was her Irish perfectionism, a mixed-blessing trait that has survived another several generations. It was vital to Grandmother to be correct in both thought and speech. In her late eighties, having partially lost her eyesight, thus her ability to read, she would listen to the radio. If the San Francisco radio announcer made a grammatical error, she would call the station. Several times in the last month, while listening to our Public Radio station, I have heard the word "intergrate." There is no such word in the English language. The word is "integrate." I so much want to pick up the phone.

No doubt both the intellectual acuity and perfectionism were critical to her emotional survival in her family of origin. A clue to this family trait comes from Welsh cathedral history. The Newport Cathedral history includes a description of her brother Alfred Edwin Monahan, who became Bishop of Monmouth in 1940. "He was a firm churchman of authoritarian personality who attracted and repelled according to taste…" Her brother William was a Canon in the Episcopal Church and wrote in three volumes The Moral Theology of St. Thomas Aquinas. Her brother Charles, a Methodist missionary in India, was involved in translating the Bible into Sanskrit. Her brother Thomas was ordained in the Church of England.

With a father and four brothers as clergymen, Protestant Christianity had a strong presence in her life. Long after her ability to read was gone, she would keep her mother's beloved French Bible on her lap. The inscription inside the cover reads: "Mary Hepworth July 18,1854. Demandez, et on vous donnera; cherchez, et vous trouverez; heurtez, et on vous ouvrira. Matt,VII 7" Ask, and you will receive; seek, and you will find; knock, and the door will be opened."

To me she was Grandmother, the ancient and grand lady at the head of our family Thanksgiving table, holding a roasted turkey leg in her right hand and saying, "If the Queen of England can do it, so can I."

Elizabeth Monhan "Lizzie" Thompson

Why would a kid like me have spent 10,000 hours behind the trumpet before the age of nineteen?

I could start with family and birth order. I was third male on the family totem pole, under my dad and under my brother who was five years my senior. Note the built-in sense of inferiority there, and the imperative to find my own voice and my own identity, separate from and equal in value to theirs. Dad taught me how to be a precision craftsman. Brother Richard taught me the meaning of brotherly encouragement, as well as how to fight, meaning how to fight and lose, and keep fighting. Mom taught me how to love. Each of these lessons proved invaluable, but for now I'd rather start with Bill Peron, my first trumpet teacher.

My parents took me to Bill when I was nine, after I had played for a year in the Theodore Judah Elementary School band. Bill was a magician on the instrument. His good friend (and partner in a Mexican tequila venture) was Raphael Mendez the world-acclaimed trumpet virtuoso. He and Raphael would challenge each other to see who could play an excerpt faster. In my lessons with Bill, it could be said that he blew me away, literally, with his trumpet virtuosity. Week after week he sat next to me and showed me precisely how to achieve my own virtuosity in the general areas of technique, musicality, and intonation. And he repeatedly told me in no uncertain terms that I would have to practice a lot to gain mastery.

The 30-minute lessons with Bill began with Longtones. Together we would take in a nice deep long trumpet breath, and play a long tone on a pitch that was in a comfortable tonal range. But it was more complicated than that. The sound had to start so softly that it was like a tonal shadow. From that shadow a steady crescendo would be created until both of us would be at full volume. Then came the descent. The volume would undergo a steady slow decrescendo until our tones would disappear into the realm of shadow tone. During Longtones I was required to produce the exact same pitch as Bill's, I mean the EXACT frequency of Bill's tone, so that the two tones sounded precisely like one trumpet was in the room. I learned that precise intonation required a matching of tonal timbre, volume and pitch.

Years later, when I was put to the test as Second Chair Trumpet in the National Symphony, the intonation refinements Bill taught resulted in the only compliment that I ever heard Principal Chair Trumpet Lloyd Geisler utter: "Ron has never played an out-of-tune note." Lloyd and I played over 700 concerts together.

After Longtones came Schlossberg Slurs, exercises in which the overtones (think bugle calls) of the instrument are connected without any break. There are three ways by which to execute bugle calls on a trumpet. They are to change embouchure (lip) aperture size, air speed and lip tension. If slurs are executed correctly the tonal changes are lightning fast and both tones have the same timbre. Bill was a master. All I had to do was listen carefully as he demonstrated. There was no rush. I listened to Bill for seven years.

I found out later that Max Schlossberg was the teacher of my Juilliard teacher William Vacchiano, and was responsible for Vacchiano being hired into the New York Philharmonic. Unknown to me at the time, Bill's Schlossberg Slurs were my first connection to the New York Philharmonic and Juilliard.

After Longtones and Schlossberg Slurs came Tonguing. A single note on the trumpet has three parts: The beginning (attack), the tonal body, and the release. There is a wide variety of ways to execute a single tone, many different attacks, tonal timbres and releases. Bill demonstrated mastery of them all.

The final section of each lesson with Bill was filled with demonstrations of the art of musicianship. Bill's musical heritage came from the concert band and cornet solo traditions. He polished my technique using cornet solos and cornet method books. I had to wait for Juilliard training to learn orchestral style and tonal concept.

In addition to weekly trumpet lessons, Bill Peron brought me into the Sacramento Symphony when I was fourteen, to perform beside him. On our first concert we performed Tchaikovsky's "Romeo and Juliet Overture" and Debussy's "Fêtes." The precision and emotional richness of the music were overwhelming. I was hooked.

During my trumpet lessons with Bill Peron time both stood still and disappeared in a flash. The doorbell announcing Bill's next student came way too soon. At my first Juilliard lesson, William Vacchiano asked me who had taught me to play. He didn't know of Bill Peron. He simply said: "He did a good job."

Seven hours each summer day, in the sweltering Sacramento heat, with the puddle of sweat under my chair, and the pendulum of the metronome swinging faster and faster, I inched forward. A small price to pay for social and self-identities, both enhanced by fun musical friendships, a string of first chair successes, and virtuoso solo performances in both concert bands and jazz bands. And all enabled by a profound connection to and passion for music performance, specifically trumpet performance.

And then there was the Toscanini NBC Symphony recording of Respighi's "Pines of Rome." Little did I know as a fifteen-year-old teary-eyed kid listening to my Motorola, that in two years I would be learning trumpet artistry from two members of Toscanini's New York Philharmonic trumpet section, William Vacchiano and Nathan Preger. And in four years I would be performing that same music of Tchaikovsky, Debussy, and Respighi as Second Chair Trumpet in Constitution Hall with the National Symphony of Washington, D.C.

SNIPPETS of a GRANDFATHER'S LIFE

240 40th Street, Sacramento, California

Bill Peron

Mom and Dad in Hawaii

Brother Rich in his '59 Austin Healy Sprite.

1959 TWEED SPORT COAT

There's a tweed sport coat hanging in my closet, size 44 short. A patch sewn under the inside pocket reads "BRIAR Traditional Apparel." With its 100% brown wool herringbone design it is an excellent example of classic men's apparel, and how little men's clothing has changed in one hundred years. Well, at least during the 64 years I have been wearing such a garment.

My earliest sport coat recollection involves a photo taken when I was fourteen, delivering my acceptance speech as Student Body President, Kit Carson Junior High School. I remember wondering why my friends were so impressed with my standing up and delivering a speech in front of the whole student body assembly. In my mind, they were just as smart and capable as I. It took me another three decades to understand that risk taking involves more than being technically competent. It involves the development of an "interior audience" that is unconditionally loving. I have the love of my parents and the respect of my friends to thank for that early gift.

The next tweed recollection finds my seventeen-year-old self, spending the first Saturday night of my two Juilliard years, dressed in sports coat and tie, in the audience of the New York City Center Opera's presentation of Carl Orff's *Carmina Burana*. Orff's cantata, with its pounding wild rhythms and licentious love themes, exploded in my musically virgin ears. And was still tearing my musical memory to shreds when I descended the steps into the 42nd Street subway station.

I caught the uptown train, the one that the sign

said would take me to the 116th Street Station. The "A" in the train window didn't mean anything to me, until after I ascended to the 116th Street subway station entrance and found none of the landmarks familiar. I had a sinking feeling as I recalled Duke Ellington's "Take the A Train." I was in Harlem, it was 11:30 at night, I was dressed like I was going to church, and I had put my last dime in the subway gate. The dim street lighting didn't offer any reassurance to my anxious realization. Neither did the cabbie in the Yellow Cab who stopped and asked me if I needed a ride. Before I could answer, he asked, "Got any money?" I answered, "No." He said, "Walk over to Sixth Ave. There are streetlights, go north to 125th Street, and then over to the West Side on 125th." Before he drove off, he said, "Your life isn't worth fifty cents here." I began walking.

Sixth Avenue was well lighted, and well policed. There were three policemen on each short block, one on each corner, and one mid-block. It was Saturday night. Everybody was out sitting on brownstone building steps and celebrating the evening. Even though I wasn't looking at them, I knew they were all looking at me. What on earth was a clean-cut nicely dressed teenage white boy doin' here? Mine was the only white face for the next nine blocks. As I turned west onto 125th Street I became aware of footsteps behind me. The street lighting was good. I didn't turn around, but my pace substantially increased. To my great relief after walking a block the sound of the footsteps behind stopped. I didn't turn around and I didn't slow down. By the time I reached the West Side with its familiar Broadway landmarks, I was relieved, breathing heavily and believed I had just made it through a close call in The Big Apple.

After an orchestra rehearsal, Charlie Schlueter, the primary person who befriended me at Juilliard, and I were hanging out. Charlie said, "Ron, I want to introduce you to one of my friends, Freddy Mills. He should be at his apartment. Let's check."

A little bio of Fred Mills is in order. Before coming to New York, at age sixteen Fred had been Stokowski's Principal Trumpet in the Houston Symphony. He went on to study with William Vacchiano at Juilliard. After a distinguished career in NYC, he returned to Canada, his home country, teamed up with four other brass virtuosi and founded the Canadian Brass. That brass quintet created a whole new genre of brass performance. Now there are music conservatories that have complete departments devoted primarily to brass quintet performance.

After walking up several flights of stairs in the dingy old Bronx brownstone apartment building, we arrived at Fred's door. Charlie knocked and the door opened with Fred greeting Charlie with a wide smile. "Hey Freddy, I want you to meet Ron Thompson. He's a good trumpet player." Fred looked over at me, smiled and said, "That's all we need…another good trumpet player."

Sy Platt and I performed in the Juilliard Orchestra together. I was an orchestra/musical theater player. Sy was a jazz player, an imaginative improv whiz who could fit in anywhere in the trumpet performance world. One afternoon he came in and sat next to me in the orchestra rehearsal whispering, "You won't believe the recording session I just did. You know Peter Schickele, the genius music Literature and Materials instructor here. He invented a make-believe composer, an odd son of J.S. Bach, P.D.Q. Bach. Schickele discovered P.D.Q.'s discarded manuscripts in a trash bin in North Dakota. One was a concerto for left-handed sewer flute, another was for Horn and Hardart, you know, the self-serve restaurant chain in Manhattan. I recorded P.D.Q.'s piece for proctophone, my trumpet mouthpiece tied to a latex glove…no kidding!"

On May 27, 1961, I celebrated my 19th birthday. A week later I auditioned for the Second Trumpet Chair in the National Symphony of Washington, D.C. Lloyd Geisler, the 52-year-old Principal Trumpet Chair and Assistant Conductor, did the private 1 ½ hour rigorous audition. Mr. Geisler, as I always addressed him, had a national reputation for his precise orchestral performance. He was considered one of the best in the business. Mr. Geisler selected me to be his primary trumpet sectional support for the NSO 250-concert season. I won the audition in a field of 33 players.

In the orchestra to my left, of diminutive physical stature and commando courage, sat Mister Geisler. Except for the great trumpet playing and faint odor of alcohol and cigar, it was like my sitting next to an empty chair. To my right was George Foss, a 6'4'' black-haired giant of a man, Juilliard trained like myself, and fully equipped with a brilliant mind and a wicked sense of humor.

A word of explanation: In the orchestra trumpeters don't play all the time. There are lots of "rests" in trumpet parts. The "rests" are not exactly restful. They must be counted very carefully. The precision of the next entrance depends on the accuracy of the count. There are tremendous disadvantages in being off count, especially on the trumpet, the loudest instrument in the orchestra.

The players help each other out by placing a hand on their right knee, and lifting a finger ever so slightly, thus signaling rest milestones. This practice keeps everybody safe and in step.

At a rehearsal during my first month, I encountered a 120-measure very slow tempo rest. I wasn't familiar with the piece. I was performing it for the first time, as was the case for most of the repertoire I was encountering.

I began the ultra-slow count. 1234, 2234,….. 50,2,3,4,…..100,2,3,4, At around the count of 20, I noticed neither Mr. Geisler nor George was assisting. Mine was the only finger going up and down. I kept going.

At 118 they both chuckled as they raised their trumpets for the upcoming entrance. They had not counted. They had relied on an oboe cue at measure 118. They had hazed me.

They chuckled.

I didn't.

They had trespassed on sacred ground.

National Symphony Orchestra of Washington, DC

After the rehearsal break, and after a visit to the backstage men's room, I returned to my chair. I reached in my back pocket, bringing out several inches of toilet paper which I draped over my music stand. I sat back in my chair.

George said, "What's this?"

I said, "It's for the next time I'm hazed. It's a reminder that I'm sitting between two assholes."

George laughed.

Mr. Geiser didn't.

It's 11:30 PM. I've just gotten home from playing a two-and-a-half hour concert at Constitution Hall, as Second Chair Trumpet with the National Symphony of Washington D.C. I'll have a bit to eat, change out of my white tie and tails and begin my nightly trumpet practice. I practice downstairs from midnight to 1:30AM using a special practice mute, one that has the feel of an open trumpet but reduces the volume significantly. There is a 10AM rehearsal call tomorrow, and I won't be practicing before the rehearsal. I'll need a fresh set of trumpet chops to get through the rehearsal.

It's my first year in the NSO and being fresh out of Juilliard, almost all the repertoire is new to me. This year, 1961, the National will play about 250 concerts during its thirty-nine-week season. It brings in more of its income through ticket sales than any other major American orchestra. At nineteen, I'm the youngest player in the orchestra. There are two guys who are both in their twenties, Second Chair Clarinet and the Tuba Chair. I'm guessing the average age of players in the orchestra is around forty. Socially I'm pretty far out of it. I'm here to perform and not for social connection.

In conservatory I studied the Principal Trumpet parts, not those of the Second Chair. So, I'm seeing most of the music for the first time. Much of it is standard repertoire for the orchestra. We're doing Scheherazade tomorrow. It's one of the standards for the National. Not so with me. There are some really lightning-fast fancy articulations in that piece. For now, I'll grab a sandwich and a glass of milk, change clothes, go downstairs and run through all the hard spots. I'll be careful not to over-stress my chops tonight. An hour-and-a-half of very careful practice should do it.

I always smile when I slip out of my Brooks Brothers concert suspenders.

The pattern is Elizabethan, kind of old-timey cream colored Rubenesque nudes, one on the right suspender and one on the left. When the suspenders are stretched, the nudes lose their Rubenesqueness. They're always good for a smile. They have been my companions for the first hundred concerts. I keep them around to dissolve some my performance anxiety.

In the National, the trumpet players are paid more than string players. It's because we are considered soloists. To be sure, we are soloists. There are no soft mistakes on a trumpet. There's lots of performance anxiety, especially as the season wears on and emotional resources ebb. William Vacchiano, my teacher at Juilliard, warned me. He said orchestra trumpet performance was a miserable way to make a living. I paid no attention. Now I see what he meant.

Before tonight's concert I warmed up a bit and watched the poker game. Backstage there are always two poker games going, one for low stakes and one for high. I always watch the high stakes game, because Herbie, a violinist, plays in that one. Herbie has a gambling addiction and consequently loses about 2,000 bucks a year. His poker playing is unpredictable. At any time he could have a winning hand, or could be totally faking it. You wouldn't catch me in that game, with my annual salary being $5,200. The others play with Herbie just because the odds are in their favor. Jim, a French horn player, counts on his poker winnings as reliable annual earned income. The other night Fred, one of the other French horn players, asked Herbie which he liked better, poker or sexual intercourse. Herbie said: "Poker, it lasts longer." After the final chord of each concert, even before the applause starts, there's a quiet chorus of whispers that ripples across the concert stage: "Deal me in. Deal me in."

For the first half of my performance tonight, I played all the notes correctly, but there was something missing. I know what Technicolor performance sounds like, and this was way too black and white. No Zing. In order to understand what was missing, one needs to have an understanding of the role of the Second Chair. The relationship of Second Chair to Principal is hand-in-glove. A good amount of the classical repertoire is scored for two trumpets only. The job of the Second Chair is to create a perfectly in tune hand-in-glove ensemble, with pitch accuracy to within one hertz (cycle-per-second), and ensemble accuracy (playing together) to within two milliseconds (thousandths of a second). A well-trained human ear can hear to that degree of accuracy. Certainly, I can.

Tonight, a valuable lesson was learned, one that I promised myself I would carry into trumpet performance for the rest of my career. I learned that there is a Second Chair attitude that is critical to achieving this degree of accuracy. For the first part of tonight's performance, I was playing with the attitude of a Principal. The job of Principal is to listen to the orchestra as a whole, and to fit perfectly into the larger ensemble, especially to the sounds of other Principal players. Because the trumpet has such a commanding timbre, it often leads the whole orchestra. If played well, its tonal presence can inspire the whole orchestra to play courageously. That's what I was doing. I was listening carefully to my own playing, and fitting my sound into that of the orchestra as a whole. The problem, as I later understood, was that there were two Principal trumpet players. Whoops! Wrong! No cigar!

Confused, frustrated and searching for a solution, my musical intuition kicked in, directing my attention to the tone coming from the player sitting next to me, that of Lloyd Geisler (whom I always address as Mr. Geisler). At age fifty-two, Mr. Geisler is one of the finest Principal Trumpet players in the nation. For the remainder of tonight's concert my whole white-hot musical focus was redirected onto Mr. Geisler's playing, His tonal production, His intonation, His ensemble. We performed our separate parts as if both parts were being performed on one instrument. Perfectly matched. And as if by magic, Technicolor Zing appeared. The trumpet parts sparkled with tonal vibration. The orchestra ensemble jelled tightknit around the inspired trumpet section. The fortissimo finale of Beethoven's Seventh Symphony brought the Constitution Hall audience of two thousand to their feet applauding in jubilant appreciation.

And I learned a performance attitude that could be experienced so clearly in a high-level professional setting. I learned that my role was to totally give over my performance focus in support of the Principal and, through trumpet sectional excellence, inspire the whole orchestra to actualize the musical brilliance and love of the composer.

Brooks Brothers Concert Attire

Ed was a crusty fifty-year-old son-of-a-bitch. He thought being the National Symphony's personnel manager, as well as the bass trombone and senior member of the brass section, gave him free rein to share his venom at will. At 20, and by far the youngest member of the orchestra, I looked like an easy target. Wrong.

As I walked off the stage after a morning rehearsal, Ed said, "Sonny, can I buy some short pants for you?" Instinctively and angrily I shot back, "If you know what's good for you, you'll watch your mouth." He smiled and walked off. He said nothing to me for the remainder of the performance season.

The next summer he hired me to be the Principal Trumpet for Carter Barron Amphitheater, with its tranquil setting in Rock Creek Park and its musically demanding schedule. Each week a new performing company or artist took the stage. Mitzi Gaynor, Harry Belafonte, Johnny Mathis, New York City Ballet, Louis Armstrong, Henry Mancini.

At each Monday morning rehearsal, I would see and play the music for the first time. That evening we would perform the first of seven shows. I had to save my trumpet lip (chops) for the show, so only the hard spots were practiced.

Ed hired another trumpet player, Dick Smith, to play second chair for the New York City Ballet performances at Carter Barron. I had not met Dick but knew him by reputation. I had won Dick's chair in the National two years earlier after he retired. His reputation was resplendent with stories of his sexcapades.

On Wednesday night of the New York City Ballet run, a young Scandinavian-looking blond beauty, wearing a fire engine red dress, sat in the front row.

Dick had trouble focusing on his music, the line of sight from the orchestra pit being a bit revealing . From the time he took his chair in the orchestra, throughout the performance, and at every chance he got, he would excitedly whisper about this enticing young blond in the red dress in the front row.

I let him hang himself.

As the final applause died down I said, "Dick… she's my wife."

During the summer of '60, as a student at Tanglewood, the Principal Trombonist of the Boston Symphony shared his wisdom with me. "Always arrive at an orchestra service at least 30 minutes early." I have invariably adhered to his advice.

At age 19 and during my first season with the National Symphony Orchestra, I arrived 30 minutes early for the evening concert performance. Grabbing the last legal parking spot close to Constitution Hall, I parked my black '59 Volkswagen bug. How lucky to have found a spot.

I reached into the rear seat to get ahold of my trumpet case. It was not there. I knew in a flash that I had left it on the sidewalk, making room for my passenger Ra's viola, and for Wayne, my other passenger whom I was about to welcome on board. My trumpet was (maybe) in Southeast Washington D.C., 30 minutes away… one way. The downbeat of the concert would be in 30 minutes.

Ra and Wayne did a quick exit, and I took off.

The trumpet case was waiting patiently for me, on the sidewalk where I had placed it. Now the concert was in 15 minutes. Again, off I went. The return trip took 13 minutes. It included going through four red lights and right down Pennsylvania Avenue, past the White House, at 60 miles an hour, with all the hypervigilance of a Grand Prix racecar driver.

Breathless and in white tie and tails, I made my way to my chair in the trumpet section just as the Principal Oboist sounded the "A" to tune the orchestra.

While I caught my breath, George, the third chair trumpet player, performed the first eight bars of my part in the overture. I took over on bar nine.

'59 VW Bug

My grandnephew Walker Thompson needed some help with his Berkeley High School paper on famous musicians. So out of the blue he called me asking if I had ever performed with famous musicians, and if so, who were they? I rattled off a couple dozen names, including those of three former San Francisco Symphony conductors. Growing up in the San Francisco vicinity he might have found those names of interest. I'm thinking Henry Mancini and "Pink Panther" were the two names that made it through the generation gap of name recognition. Walker loves jazz, being a trombonist himself, so my story of doing a shared concert of "Third Stream Music" with the Count Basie Orchestra embedded in the National Symphony was "cool."

Anytime I catch myself reflecting on those years I spent in the NSO, I think of my performing in a concert that Pierre Monteux conducted, a program of French masterpieces, including La Mer and Daphnis et Chloe Suite No. 2. Monteux was born in 1875 and died in 1964, a year after my peak experience with him. Pierre conducted with smiling eyes and a super-clear baton. The orchestra had never played Daphnis et Chloe so slowly and with such sensual rhythmic precision. It was like slow lovemaking. No. It was slow lovemaking.

The ocean had always been my friend. The warm California sun-filled days of my childhood, building sandcastles on the beach at Santa Cruz, my early adolescence solo bodysurfing the Pacific waters off Pismo Beach, the swimming barefoot out a half-mile beyond the surf, to be with the skin divers as they explored the undersea forests of giant kelp. My head bobbing out there like that of a sea lion. And the undersea spearfishing in the wild coves of Northern California. Ocean Cove, Timber Cove, Ruth Carlson Cove.

So as a freshly married young adult vacationing at Rehobeth Beach, Delaware, I couldn't wait to bodysurf the beckoning Atlantic waters. It was a bright warm day with plenty of surf, a great bodysurfing day. I did notice that the wave patterns were different than those of the Pacific. More choppy. Closer together. My first few bodysurfings rivaled any of my Pacific experiences. I caught the peak of the swells, and swimming full strength with a slightly arched back, rode those babies all the way to where the frothy edge meets the warm wet sand.

Hooked, out I went to catch another wave.

Early in my Pacific Ocean bodysurfing experience I learned two important lessons. The first is to never turn your back on the ocean. The surf is full of surprises. The second is that there are two basic wave shapes. The first is a roller. The wave gradually releases its energy evenly, as it approaches the beach. Rollers make for great bodysurfing. The other type is the planter. It is named that because it plants your head in the sand.

It's dangerous as hell. As the receding wave returns the approaching wave is lifted high and vertically comes crashing down, carrying its catch of anything, including the body of a surfer pointing like an arrow at the wet sand below.

My next Atlantic wave was a planter. As I went over the barrel into the surging freefall. I instinctively relaxed, which likely saved my life. I was a second away from learning how far my neck could bend without breaking. I came up dazed, my head stinging. There was blood. In the seconds before the next wave I yelled for help, frantically waving at the distant lifeguard. He was sitting in his lifeguard chair talking with some girls. He waved back. I dove into the next oncoming wall of water, bobbing up a little farther out and knowing I was on my own.

There was another threat. The wave angle was pushing me ever closer to a breakwater that extended a couple hundred yards out into the ocean. I knew I was a goner if I got smashed onto those massive cement blocks. I had one option. Swim out to sea. After negotiating another dozen waves, I found myself swimming in open water beyond the breakwater. More floating than swimming I slowly made my way to the deep swells on the safe side of the breakwater. I remember getting close to shore, catching a blessed roller and it carrying me all the way to the waiting warm sand.

1964 NATIONAL CATHEDRAL

It was a slow climb up the dark tunnel, its stone steps leading to the very top of the newly completed Gloria in Excelsis central tower of the National Cathedral. I was glad I was small in stature. My right elbow rubbed against the unforgiving cold stone wall. I was reminded of my spelunking days as an adventuresome adolescent. There were four of us making the climb, the trumpet section of the National Symphony. We carried two-foot long-belled fanfare trumpets, supplied by the cathedral, with which we would be broadcasting fanfares from the highest perch, celebrating the newly completed 300-foot central tower.

Caught in traffic, I was last to arrive on the job. I ended up with the worst of the four trumpets. When I picked it up, the bell came off in my hand. I shoved it back in place, feeling more than a little concern.

From our narrow perch atop the cathedral tower we could see for miles. The sunny spring day allowed a broad vista of Washington D.C., all the way to the distant Washington Monument.

The rest of the orchestra was seated on a platform several hundred feet directly below us. A perfect vertical line of sight from my position.

What if that bell came off during the performance? It could kill somebody. I undid my shoelace and tied it firmly to both the trumpet valve casing and the bell.

It did come off during the second fanfare, the bell dangling back and forth like a kid's yoyo. I jammed it back on and finished the final set of fanfares without a hitch. On the way back down the narrow staircase no one said anything. I don't remember retying my shoelace. I do remember being exceedingly relieved for having prevented a likely tragedy.

National Cathedral, Washington, DC

A while back I listed the incidents in my 82 years of life when I was in real danger of losing my life. I admit this might seem like a strange thing to do, but no stranger than some of the 43 incidents on the list. There was the time I nearly broke my neck bodysurfing in the Atlantic, or the time as kids my older brother and I shot at each other with our 22's. Yes, 22 caliber rifles. There was no danger, because we were at quite a distance apart and we were "just shooting blanks." And then there was a five-year period when as an electrical engineer I worked in a high-voltage lab. Most of the test circuits, in their fully charged state, were lethal. I counted the five years in the lab as one item on my danger list.

The incident that I'm about to describe was carried out in response to a George Washington University Physics class project in which I was asked to build something that illustrated Newtonian mechanics. At 22 years of age, I had just resigned from the National Symphony of Washington D.C. and was beginning my career as an electrical engineer. Mortality had not entered my consciousness.

Out back in my garage I designed, built and tested a ballistic pendulum. That is a device used to measure the muzzle velocity of a bullet, how fast the bullet comes out of the barrel of a gun. I owned a 22-caliber pistol, and I thought a ballistic pendulum would be an interesting way to satisfy the project requirement. The professor did not know about my choice until I handed in the final report.

The design consisted of a 30 inch tall wooden frame, which supported a kid's swing-like 18 inch pendulum. A 6x1.5-inch pipe, filled with modeling clay and capped with a pipe cap (to stop the bullet) was fastened to the tip of the pendulum arm. The assembly swung freely back and forth. Fastened to the pendulum pipe was a razor blade. Attached to the side of the test frame was a sheet of tissue paper mounted in an old picture frame.

Theoretically the test procedure was to work as follows: Discharge the bullet into the tail end of the pipe, which would cause the pipe to move forward in the pendulum arc pattern. The razor blade would cut an arc pattern in the mounted tissue paper. By using the several mass/arc height variable values and Newtonian formulas, the muzzle velocity value would be determined.

The short ending to the story is that it worked. My test value was 1100ft/sec. The manufacturer's published value was 1130ft/sec.

The long ending to the story is about the first test shot blowing the clay and pipe cap out the end, spraying clay all over the garage wall, and the bullet ricocheting God knows where.

I stacked three US silver quarters in the end of the second clay-filled newly capped pipe. Fired a second volley and, voila, it worked. No splatter. The bullet was contained within the test pipe. The measurements were taken from the slit in the tissue paper. The test results were calculated.

The professor gave me an A+. His only comment was: "Curiosity killed a cat."

It was a sun-filled idyllic morning at the California beach as my two-year-old daughter, Elise, and I spread our big striped towel on the sparsely populated sandy beach. She immediately busied herself with her little blue plastic sand bucket and red sand shovel, filling and dumping. A squadron of white pelicans floated by, inches above the crest and trough of a mild surf. I settled back onto the beach towel, closed my eyes, taking in the salty aroma of the Pacific Ocean and musing a loose mixture of random thoughts.

I don't know what prompted me to open my eyes, but I did. She wasn't there.

A quick super-vigilant scan spotted her, running pell-mell as fast as her little chubby legs could carry, dangerously close to the surf edge.

Off I went, tight fists piston-pounding. A tenth of a second seemed like a year.

Just as she fell forward, her face submerged in the receding wave, my hands grabbed, pulling her wet body out, and holding her tightly to my chest.

She said, "WHEEEEEEEEE."

It was in the '60's. We were both in our twenties, recently graduated, and both project engineers, when our Director of Engineering summoned Jess and me into his office. "Our sales staff have committed us to an interesting project. The corner-office big guy says he wants you and Jess to take it on. Here's the specs."

Jess and I had a look. Page three described the test waveform (the intrusive foreign overvoltage surge from which protection was needed) and the spec response time of the overvoltage arrester prototype which needed to be invented. Our company's bread and butter sales came from our line of electrical surge protection equipment, including airliner lightning protectors and telephone sparkgap voltage-overload arresters. The waveform at which we were looking was much faster than anything we had previously seen. And the electrical current follow-through was huge. We were both thinking the same thing: "Holy Shit!"

He said there would be some challenges. We would have to come up with our own new test circuits and setups, noting that the bank of capacitors would likely fill a space approximately five hundred cubic feet.

I said, "What about the wavefront? That's faster than our monitoring oscilloscopes."

He answered, "We'll get new scopes. Oh…a couple more challenges: There's no daytime lab hours available. You'll have to work at night. And… Sales has promised our customers a working prototype in 90 days. It's for Electromagnetic Pulse….nuclear."

"I wish I could tell you that you have a choice about taking this on. I can't."

The design of the full-load test circuit dictated how the high-voltage capacitors would be oriented in order to generate the test spec waveform. This circuit design meant that if one capacitor shorted, the entire electrical energy of the test circuit would be dumped into the shorted capacitor, causing a potential massive explosion. We understood the risk. At least we thought we understood the risk.

Our shop built our design prototypes during the day. Jess and I tested them at night, meticulously filling our lab notebooks with test data, design configurations and materials research. This was new territory for our engineering department and for us. A play-for-keeps Tom Edison project. Logical step after logical step, design failure after design failure, we edged toward our goal. Within the final two weeks, Jess and I, miles beyond exhaustion, arrived at a design that met specs. Eureka!

Hypervigilance is a life-saving attribute for working in a high-voltage laboratory. Any physical contact with test circuits is done one-handed. If a mistake is made, either due to fatigue or miscalculation, one wants the electrical shock current to run down the side of the body through the foot to the floor, and not through the heart. At one point Roy, one of lab techs, showed me the scarred hole in the bottom of his foot.

Midway through the project the only remaining patience Jess and I had was with the technical challenge of the project and with each other.

Every morning at 2:45am the employee break bell, which rang every 12 hours and hung on the wall of the lab, would go off, shattering our concentration and scaring the hell out of us. Invariably it would happen just as one of us would be reaching in to adjust a high voltage test circuit. One night Jess and I looked at each other. I got the ladder. He got the hammer. He climbed the ladder and beat the goddamned bell right off the wall. The only evidence that remained was two small protruding naked wires.

Throughout the development phase the test circuit performed flawlessly. Sometime during the night before the final design review, as we raced to complete the last prototype full-load test, one of the high-voltage capacitors shorted out. From an adjoining room, I heard the explosion and saw Jess' tight fists pumping up and down as he sprinted across the lab floor, away from the exploded capacitor bank, and the capacitor oil dripping from the lab's sixteen-foot ceiling.

The next morning, at the design review meeting, the customer's four senior engineers pored over our data and smiled seasoned smiles at our reporting of the previous night's unwanted surprise. They also liked our design, but not enough to award us with the contract.

Years later I was told that our customer had a reputation for stealing designs.

High Voltage Switch Electrodes (post discharge)

Sometimes vignettes speak volumes.

It was in the last hour of a rare visit by my preteen daughter Kirsten. She said, "Dad, I want your help with something." She went on to say that her stepfather's brother, who was living in her household, had personal habits (including smoking cigarettes) which were in conflict with the values of her family. He had overstayed his welcome and no one knew how, or was willing, to ask him to leave.

In that hour I taught her the basics of Rosenberg's Nonviolent Communication. With a look of relief she said, "Thanks, Dad."

On our next phone call she reported returning to her Plano, Texas home, and confronting the brother, who moved out having heard the clear message of his unwelcomed presence.

Kirsten was eleven.

On another of our many phone calls, this time eight years later, Kirsten shared her story of her experience in the airport at Riyadh, Saudi Arabia. She was in line to check in, after having visited her mother who was living in Saudi Arabia at that time. A middle-aged Saudi man butted in line directly in front of her. She told him that he couldn't do that, and that he would have to go to the end of the line. In Saudi Arabia, women, especially young women, and especially in public, are not allowed to tell middle-aged Saudi men what to do (where to go).

He went to the end of the line.

Kirsten

The Pacific Coast to the west of Santa Barbara is dotted with stretches of sandy beaches and rocky shoreline. Twice I've climbed out to the white-water edge of the rocky outcropping that defines the western boundary of Refugio Beach. First my mother's ashes found their home there, and years later my dad's. It was the right place because of their ashes being together, because the California Coast brought them so much joy, and because of the timelessness of the ocean.

My friend and mentor, Dan, was in his mid-eighties when I first met him at All Saints By The Sea Episcopal Church. Sporting a full head of gray hair and standing well over six feet, his relaxed gentility and steady gaze drew my attention right away. The Second Fact I learned about him was that when Dan was just a kid his father died attempting to save a drowning child in a swollen river. This became explanation enough for why Dan held principled living to be more important than life itself.

At that time I was Director of Auxiliary Services at Westmont College, an evangelical Christian institution located in Montecito, California, a couple miles up the road from All Saints. One of my duties was to manage the college bookstore. The store employed a couple dozen Westmont students, one of whom, a bright young junior, came into my office requesting my counsel. She wanted to become an ordained Christian minister and was being discouraged by the clergy of her denomination and her evangelical peers. Because she was female. She wanted my opinion and, no doubt, my encouragement. I told her I had just the person with whom she needed to talk. I arranged for her to meet Dan that very afternoon, after telling him of the challenges she faced.

The First Fact I had learned about Dan was that he was the retired Episcopal Bishop of Colorado. The Third Fact was that he was one of the three Episcopal bishops who, in July of 1974, were the first to ordain women (the "Philadelphia Eleven") to the Episcopal priesthood, blasting apart a 250-year tradition of the Church and violating its Canons. Two years later, in September of

1976, the Canons were changed to include provisions for the ordination of women. I made sure that my young employee knew all about Dan's bold contribution in elevating the role of women in the Episcopal Church.

We met in the walnut paneled library of the administration building. For two hours the young lady and I listened while Dan told of his life as an Episcopal priest and social activist.

His first assignment was to minister to the Native Americans living in a remote village in northern Wisconsin. He told of going to his bishop, soon after being assigned, to request a change of placement. It was too difficult. The "Indians" were too set in their ways to be receptive to The Gospel. His bishop said the assignment demanded a priest who was open-minded and had tenacity of faith, and to give it a bit more time. Dan was there ten years. He was the only person from outside the tribe who knew the way, by footpath and canoe, through the bog to the village. Dan told us the Native Americans taught him everything he knows about spirituality.

He told of getting off the plane to join Martin Luther King and the human rights march. At the bottom of the ramp, he was met by a State Trooper who pointed his pistol at Dan, telling him to get back on the plane. Dan said, "Son, go ahead and shoot me if you have to, but I'm not getting back on that plane." And he walked on past the Trooper.

While serving in the Diocese of Baltimore, he became aware of an injustice. The Church had longstanding ownership of valuable harbor real estate, the income from which was siphoned off to build lovely churches

     SNIPPETS of a GRANDFATHER'S LIFE

in the wealthy suburbs, leaving the needs of the harbor area poor unmet. Dan organized the harbor residents sufficiently to take political control of the diocesan income and redirect it toward the previously unmet housing needs. When Dan was telling us of this social activism I remember thinking, "This guy is a modern day Robin Hood."

The range wars were raging when Dan became the Bishop of Colorado, cattlemen vs. sheep ranchers. Escalation and firearms were afoot. Dan arranged for men of both camps to meet with him. Sitting across the table from each other, with Dan at the head, he told them, in no uncertain terms that the issues were going to be settled peacefully in that room and in that meeting. Dan was able to broker a truce. Toward the end of the successful talks the fire bell was heard by all present. One horror-struck rancher looked across the table and told a cattleman, "I ordered your barn be burned. I'll double any loss you suffer today."

Our time with Dan went by quickly. We both thanked him profusely for sharing his life stories with us and wished him God's love. And in true Episcopal form he said, "And also with you."

My young friend thanked me and said she had received all the inspiration she needed to move toward ordination after graduation.

I told her I had one more story about Dan: that Dan and his wonderful wife Elizabeth, had invited me, my wife Maggie and my two daughters Betsy and Sylvia to dinner at their retirement residence, Samarkand. As the waiter took our orders, he had a quiet exchange with Dan. To my kids' delight and wide-eyed surprise our first course was a dish of ice cream. Dan explained, "Life is short. It's important to eat dessert first." From that time forth Betsy and Sylvia have remembered Dan Corrigan as the bishop who ate his dessert first.

Dessert First

1986 OLD MISSION SANTA BARBARA

Set in a window frame of our old Vermont farmhouse is a full-color photograph of the Santa Barbara Old Mission. The Old Mission was across from our home on Garden Street. At one time our property was the Mission olive grove. From time to time, I'd take my two young Korean-born daughters over to the Mission steps to play. One of our favorites was to do an evening visit, when the front façade spotlights lit up the grand entrance and adobe twin towers. We'd dance up and down the tiers of steps directly in front of the several spotlights, projecting our giant silhouetted shadows onto the Mission façade.

Sometimes we'd stroll over under the afternoon sun and sit on the walls of the round wishing well fountain, which has graced the expansive frontal grounds for centuries. My two daughters, now fully into their adulthood, readily remind me of the time I added to my coin collection by getting my right hand and arm wet.

The sanctuary of The Old Mission was the location of the only solo trumpet recital of my life. I've assisted on many; however, I've performed only one in which I soloed on every selection. I sent a recording to my Juilliard trumpet instructor William Vacchiano, who in a return note said it was the best thing he'd heard all year. That comment will stay with me for the rest of my life.

Old Mission Santa Barbara

As I sat in a front-row folding chair to listen to the Music Academy of The West Brass Ensemble rehearsal, a gentleman with an air of casual refinement sat down in the empty chair next to mine. I recall his shirt to be a patterned soft grey linen. His trousers may have been linen as well. As he sat, he smiled at me a gentle smile. A full head of white hair pegged him to be about seventy. I found out much later that he was ninety-two. He placed a cordovan glove leather satchel on the floor between his legs as he relaxed into his seat.

Midway through the rehearsal, the conductor, a renowned classical trombone soloist and pedagogue, signaled for a break. My new neighbor reached into his leather bag and took out what appeared to be a stack of music manuscripts. He stood and walked toward the podium in an attempt to get the conductor's attention. He succeeded, but only briefly, as the conductor, apparently not interested in the manuscripts, brushed him off with an air of irritation. A wrinkled brow signaling disappointment accompanied my gentleman as he returned to his seat and put the stack carefully back into its leather home.

The rehearsal being completed, I offered my hand to the gentleman and introduced myself, throwing out a trumpet performance credential or two. He introduced himself, Loren Luper, and responded mentioning that he had been the solo chair trombonist with the Sousa Band.

So... I was talking with THE trombone soloist of THE John Philip Sousa Concert Band.

After a moment of hesitation, I asked to see what he had brought in his satchel. As he reached down, he explained it was a hand-copied manuscript of many of the solos he performed with the Sousa band. The handwork was that of a "Czech clarinetist", another member of the band. My eyes widened as he revealed page after page of music manuscript that had more the appearance of calligraphy than band music. And certainly not trombone music. This had to be violin music. I had never seen so many stratospheric black notes on a trombone part in my life. Being aware of my surprise, he assured me it was normal fare.

I told him straight away that he had a treasure there, and that I wanted to meet again to talk about how he could publish. This time his eyes widened. We agreed to meet the next afternoon.

His home was modest and immaculate, his wife welcoming, on the athletic side, and it turned out, thirty years his junior. She provided freshly baked sugar cookies and a tea that I recognized as a smoky Lapsang Souchong. As we sat at the sunlit Formica breakfast table, he brought out concert band photos, all yellowed with age and scribbled with signatures. Several famous concert bands were represented, Sousa, Gilmore, Conway, Loren's young face easily recognizable.

And there were band stories: how Gilmore, or was it Conway, was the real conductor on some of the Sousa Band's wax recordings. I assured him that there was plenty of material for a book: manuscript, photos and personal recollections. All of interest, unique and valuable.

Another of my surprises was finding out Loren's age, 92. His slim face and youthful skin were deceptive. I asked his secret. He said he ate a banana every night before bed.

And he said he had been depressed for a year. "Couldn't shake it." Said this was the first time in a long time he had felt joy. As we parted it was clear that Loren had found a path to his passion. Within five months he published his book, his personal opus, filled with authenticity and musical value.

At six months I got a grief-filled angry call from his wife. Loren had died. A quick death. An aneurism. It was Sunday morning, and he was at the breakfast table. A minute later he was dead. She reasoned the rigorous activity and emotional pressure of writing the book had taken him from her. It was all my fault.

I acknowledged her grief as real and raw. My inner thoughts and emotions were quietly different. Loren died as he would have wanted to die. Filled with fresh, creative joy.

1992 CANTERBURY PARK

During the summer of 1992 I was the Official Hornblower at Canterbury Park Racetrack, located just outside of Minneapolis. I performed The Call To Post 242 times that summer, 241 times perfectly.

Canterbury Park is a full-blown horse country thoroughbred racetrack. The huge multi-sectioned battleship gray stadium holds thousands of excited horserace fans of all ages. The massive structure is crowned by rows of brightly colored pennants which wave in the soft Minnesota summer breeze. Everything is manicured, the grounds, the luxuriant horse barns, even the acres of freshly painted parking lots. The track itself, with its row of claustrophobic starting gate cages, looks more like a giant board game than anything real. But real it is, and it is where I came to do eleven performances each Saturday, one performance at the beginning of each race.

My job was to formally announce the race by playing The Call To Post twice. I did this just as the line of horses, with jockeys suited up in distinctive silks, were directed down the path to the starting gate. My cue was when the first horse and jockey appeared. I stood on a small platform centered directly in front and at the base of the stadium. I was decked out in full classic Hornblower uniform, red topcoat, black hat, white jodhpurs and shiny leather riding boots. The bell of my long herald trumpet was held six inches away from a microphone which, when I discharged, sent the familiar and anxiously awaited Call To Post out to every corner of the stadium.

After several Saturdays I began to notice the children out in front of my platform. They gathered to see me and hear the call up close. I was bothered by my observation that no adult was paying any attention to them. In fact, they were quite a young scraggly bunch, some without shoes. On subsequent Saturdays I began to let one at a time up on the platform to "help me" hold my herald trumpet. Their delight was amazing. Soon I had a line waiting. One Saturday my young daughter Betsy came to the racetrack with me and organized the kids, taking reservations for all eleven races, and helping the younger ones up to the platform. The kids were so well behaved that I began letting multiples hold the horn. I found I could accommodate up to four at a time.

In the stadium gift shop I spied jockey cards, a takeoff on baseball cards, and soon began giving each child a jockey card after their turn holding the horn. That was the frosting on the cake. The kids had found their point of interest, and I had found a way to infuse my performances with loving social intent. I knew that loving social intent would reduce my performance anxiety and enhance my performance accuracy.

Just before one race I assembled a quartet of young horn holders, with the child closest to the trumpet bell being one of the cutest little blond six-year-old girls in the world. As always, I took care to instruct each of them to hold steady during the sudden loud blast of the call. Even a slight jarring of the instrument would derail the delicate balance of the mouthpiece on my lips and send out something that would be far less than desirable.

The first horse and jockey appeared. My white-hot performance focus took over. And the inevitable occurred. The littlest angel jerked just enough to upset the apple cart. The first call was a loud blur of noises in the rhythm of The Call To Post. They must have heard it a mile away. The immediate second call was perfect. I responded like nothing had happened, handed out the jockey cards and warmly thanked each child for helping.

As I moved through the crowd toward the gift shop to replace my supply of jockey cards, in conspicuous attire and holding my noisemaker, I was met by smiling face after smiling face.

Jockey Cards

The following statement was delivered in person, and as part of a panel, to Episcopalians at three forum locations in the Philadelphia area in November of 2006. The intent of the statement was to lay a groundwork for understanding the panel's reporting of the clergy sexual abuse coverup perpetrated by their Bishop, Charles Bennison. Earlier that year, the Chief Investigative Journalist from ABC News in San Francisco aired a documentary revealing multiple instances of clergy sexual abuse perpetrated by John Bennison, an Episcopal Priest and Charles' brother. Charles role was revealed as well. When Concerned Pennsylvania Episcopalians (CPE) first learned about their bishop's role in the coverup, they put out an invitation to those whose lives were affected by the abuse and coverup. Six spoke their truths at the forums: a psychologist who provided context for understanding the complexities of clergy sexual abuse, the former wife of the perpetrator, the mother and brother of the youngest victim/survivor (13 at the time the abuse began), a former youth group member who was being groomed to be the next victim, and a priest advocate for victims of clergy sexual abuse.

Ron's Opening Statement for the Forums on Clergy Sexual Abuse Coverup

The last time I visited Philadelphia, a little over forty years ago, it was under quite different circumstances than those of this visit. I had just completed a three-month preparation for an audition for the Philadelphia Orchestra. Standing on the stage of The Academy of Music, I was going after one of those rare chairs in the trumpet section of that fine orchestra. I have long since forgiven Eugene Ormandy for choosing a musician with far more experience and maturity than I. But for me, this critical incident left an indelible imprint. It was the first time in my young musical life that I had lost an audition. After forty years, I have a vivid recall of details of the experience. It certainly changed my view of the world, and of my place in it.

Today you will be introduced to material which left indelible imprints on the lives of those on this panel and many others. Many of the events happened years ago but are vividly present in their memories.

As I look at each of you, I am impressed with the importance of the material and issues which will be presented and discussed here today. As you may know, I am the husband of Maggie Thompson, who is the former wife of John Bennison and the former sister-in-law of Chuck Bennison, your present bishop. Maggie and I have been together for twenty-nine years. That area of my life seems to have gone by very rapidly and joyously. We chose inter-country adoption to create a family and we are in the twenty-second year of that process. Interwoven into our family, marital and personal lives are histories of abuse: emotional, physical, sexual, and spiritual.

Today, in this room, I trust that we are not going to question whether abuse, and in particular clergy sexual abuse and its coverup, are damaging. They most certainly are. The resulting trauma does not end with the cessation of the acts themselves. Whether a person is abused as a child, an adolescent, or an adult, that person is likely to experience long-term effects that interfere to some degree with day-to-day functioning. In the case of clergy sexual abuse the effects are particularly insidious. Such abuse damages the victim's spiritual identity as well as self-identity.

The very people who are entrusted with building a helpful, even essential, loving internal divine audience that is one's vision of God, serve up a destructive non-life affirming vision of God. Rather than building loving creative souls, they damage and destroy the souls of those whom they abuse. And they destroy the divine mission of the church as well. In the case of Episcopal clergy who abuse, the vision of Jesus the divine Christ is reduced to a myth, worthy only of cynical distrust.

On the top of the list of reasons for my being here is my provision of support for Maggie, even as she places herself in a position of vulnerability. It would be a gross understatement to say that I admire her social intent, intellect and courage, as she tells her truth. I hold identical admiration for the others who are before you today on this panel.

I would hope that there are none in this gathering who would pose the question to Maggie, or any other abuse survivor: "If you knew all about this why didn't you tell?"

Such a question, even if well intended, shows a gross ignorance of the dynamics of abuse. Suffice it to say that victims never know the full extent of the perpetrator's thought process or behavioral patterns. The perpetrator preys on the fears and naiveté of the victim, and manipulates with partial-truth reasoning, secrecy, and deceit. He reduces the horizon of choice as he spins his web of lies. The most fundamental lie, the biggest lie of abuse, is that the victim does not possess choice. During the abuse phase, the victim is not an empowered choice-maker.

The perpetrator is caught in a similar web of lies. In his internal world, he must have, or is entitled to, his object of obsession, whether it is his position of social status, his social-spiritual influence, his sexual domination, or his sexual stimulation ecstasy.

The primary missing link in the process is "social interest," the social orientation of intending to raise the quality of life for others. There was a time I can recall, when this was commonly called "Christianity." Put simply, the perpetrator's social conscience – his empathy for others – has not been developed.

Some of today's material will be painful to hear, and painful to present as well. Maggie and I and the others before you have lived with the emotional fallout of these critical events for decades Almost all of you will be hearing this material for the first time.

I want expectations and boundaries to be clear. We are here to tell our truth of what happened and share the personal impact on some of the lives of those affected. During the conversation and discussion time, we will do our best to provide clarification of our material. Our focus is on building empathy for and with the people of the Diocese of Pennsylvania. We are not here to argue. We are here to educate and clarify.

Our expectation and understanding of the role of the media professionals present is to document and report this process as accurately as possible and certainly not to dominate or impede.

We are not a formal organization. We have no sponsor. Unless contributions come from other sources, the cost of this effort (an estimated $5,000) will be paid by Margo, Andy, Julia, Susan, Maggie and myself.

Much of my personal focus here will be on developing empathy for you as you listen and respond. I expect a full range of responses, from anger and denial to deep empathic sadness and anxiety. I ask you to agree with me that though the human needs and feelings expressed in this material are universal, each of us will have our own unique reaction to it. Please listen to what actually happened, as free from moral evaluation as possible. Try to imagine the feelings of all the people involved. Look for the human needs in the context of each situation, needs such as safety, respect, belonging, trust, peace, sexual expression. Identify the strategies by which each person attempted to get his or her needs met, and the social effects, the effects on others, of those strategies.

And finally, please agree with me that this material is being given to you as a gift, a truth-telling that is not meant to be a demand, but rather an invitation for you to create an empathic, non-punishing, life-affirming response for yourself and for all the people of your Diocese.

The Full Monty is among the masterpieces of musical theater. Its plot illuminates the desperation of a bunch of unemployed blue-collar male workers as they hatch a plan to do a strip show to earn money to meet the pressing needs of their families. The show's hard-driving big band jazz score is written so exquisitely that it's easy for the musicians to outdo themselves. This is musical theater at its best.

The climax of the show occurs during its last seconds, when the houselights come on (for one second only) and the G-strings come off, flung with abandon high into the air, revealing…well…the full montys.

On opening night at our opera house, I sat in the lead trumpet chair in the orchestra pit facing the conductor. I had no view of the stage, but to the left of the conductor I could see the reactions of a middle-aged couple seated in the front row.

It was a sterling performance. The band nailed the chart. The guys on stage were amazing. Better than at any of the rehearsals.

As the show's climax approached, the deep darkness which enveloped the stage suddenly gave way to bright illumination.

The houselights were on. The G-strings were flung high in the air.

And the lights stayed on. And the lights stayed on.

I heard an "Oh No!" from the stage.

The lady in the front row began laughing convulsively.

The guy next to her was staring at the stage, with a look on his face as if he was seeing an Unidentified Flying Object.

One of the G-strings landed in my lap, a jeweled leather contraption.

7…8…9…Houselights Off.

Stage dark.

Curtain down.

Houselights On.

Music.

Terrycloth robed actors.

Bows.

Standing Ovation.

It's late. My wife Maggie has just slipped into bed beside me. No part of her is touching me. She is rigidly still, perfectly quiet, frozen with fear. A moment ago, on her way into bed, she gently moved the blanket, tightly held, wrapped so as to expose the large puffy bandage on the top of my head. The dressing concealed the wound, as I fitfully slept. When the blanket moved ever so slightly, I screamed.

Earlier, when she came home from choir practice, I had not told her the full story, the full truth. Now, as I deliberately chose to massage her scalp and softly run my fingers down the outside of her smooth ear, I chose to talk. My intent was to set her at ease and help her to make sense of my scream.

I told her that the surgical procedure I had chosen, and endured, earlier in the day, was more than I had expected. I had expected that a thin wafer of flesh, including the ¾-inch diameter cancer-celled area would be taken. After being given width options, I had chosen "generous margins." I wanted one operation, not several all-day trips, and not several incremental procedures.

During the surgery I had not felt any pain, except from the pricks of the anesthesia needle. But definitely I had felt the pressure of the surgeon's hands, pinching here and there, while he cut.

Before the dressing was applied, I asked to see the surgical site. The width was not the surprise. It was the depth. The surgeon and nurse held up two mirrors, so that I could get a panoramic view. There it was, a good eighth-of-an-inch-deep full moon crater, filled with a snake nest of cauterized bright-red blood veins. The instant I saw that, I both dissociated and associated. I was looking inside a head. Inside my head.

Maggie asked if I thought I had been disfigured. I hesitated. "Yes, I expect to be disfigured, but it's out of my line-of-sight. I'm short, so I expect it might be a point of interest for the taller people around me. Physically it means little to me. But mostly, the wound is psychological. There's something sacred about one's head. At least there used to be."

After a bit, she dozed off. I couldn't sleep, so I got up and read some theology.

Theology has always put me to sleep.

Something inside me invariably smiles when I think of Peter. Perhaps it was the gentleness and precision of his social presence. Perhaps it was his willingness to share his musical creativity. Perhaps it was the tender devotion he and Marcia enjoyed in their marriage.

The first thing I noticed when he joined the Christ Church (Montpelier, Vermont) choir, was that he sang in tune. The second was that I loved the service music that he composed. Still do. The third was that there was always more to learn from him and about him.

A glimpse into his accomplishments would reveal his being on the faculty of Mannes School of Music for 32 years, and his having composed and published over 300 musical works including seven symphonies, six string quartets and numerous chamber orchestra, choral and organ compositions.

Months after he and Marcia had decided to stop making the long Sunday morning trek to Christ Church, I visited their Wolcott home. Over cups of hot tea Peter and I talked about the creative process, and how Peter's creativity was set free by having his Christ-centered God of Love be his internal audience.

My wife says what I put in my stir-fry lunches is one step away from the compost bucket. She's right. The other day my daughter tossed several of her delicious Korean red bean buns in the compost bucket. The dough didn't meet her super-high standards. It met mine. I used the one-hour rule and rescued them. They became the base ingredient for the following week's vegie stir-fries. I didn't tell my daughter. I adhere closely to a long held personal value of never lying, most of the time. That personal value comes in handy often because both she and my wife find a ready source of shared humor when it comes to the contents of my vegie stir-fry lunches. Real Life Composter, even though accurate, does not fully honor my noble intent: achieving radiant health through excellent nutrition.

The first thing to be understood about the stir-fries is that they all taste the same. No matter what ingredients fill the fry pan, the flavor is dominated by the sauce mix. That's because I use the same two Korean sauces, Bibigo red made with hot Korean chilies, and Bibigo brown (soy-based marinade). I use a dedicated set of plastic squirt bottles. Six big squirts of brown and four little squirts of red. If five squirts of red are used, an entirely different dish is produced. Probably only legal in Korea. Six squirts and your tongue is cauterized. Bibigo brown has a high-octane garlic content. I'm told that the commercial airline pilots can tell when they have entered Korean airspace. Something about the aroma of garlic.

The Bibigo sauces are advertised as the most popular sauces in Korea, and for good reason. Whether their base is soy or chili, they deliver a flavor richness that I equate with the Korean soul. Beautiful, refined, strong, spirited, and direct. I can say that because I have parented two Korean-born daughters, both of whom display those qualities, and more.

Although all my stir-fries taste the same, they don't chew the same. The consistency is always different, always dependent on what goes in the fry pan. What found its way randomly into the pan this past month?

Olive oil, grape seed oil, carrots, purple cabbage, green cabbage, green onion, onion, Brussels sprouts, leftover garlic tofu, leftover wild rice, leftover shredded lettuce, leftover baked purple potato, leftover baby potato, spinach noodles, Chinese wheat noodles, Top Ramen noodles (no MSG laced powder packet), Kimchi, leftover bibimbop, leftover spaghetti, rescued Korean red bean bun, Italian parsley, fiddleheads, sunchoke, turmeric, celery, leftover tomato slice, leftover Dr. Prager Green Gardenburger, leftover whole-wheat dinner roll, leftover breakfast fried egg, leftover mesclun salad, asparagus, leftover cornbread, leftover breakfast potato pancake.

As you can see there exists a wide variety (perhaps some would say an indiscriminate variety) of ingredients. I'm very aware that I am one generation removed from the Great Depression, and a little over five from the Irish Potato Famine. So, nothing is wasted. In go handfuls, plastic freezer bags full, Tupperware containers full. However most gets collected and stored in Dad's Stir-fry Refrigerator Drawer, the contents of which quietly accumulate while family life goes on.

So, there you have it, day after day, delicious stir-fry after delicious stir-fry.

Just like life: spicy, constantly changing, and always graced with leftovers.

Stir-fry

Stir-Fry

Our Creator, who exists in the place of light without limit, whose light is the pivot point upon which all of creation turns, and whose ruling vision, consent, and joy arises in nature even as a host of stars brings its unlimited brilliance to the firmament, give to us this day our daily empathic understanding. Set us free from our errors and frustrated hopes, as we seek to set free those who are in error against us. Counsel us so as to avoid that which would tempt us to be out of rhythm with your vision for us. For your counsel and guidance are empowerment and pure delight, now and forever. Amen

For years I couldn't forgive others for their grievous, even tragic, self-serving, mean behaviors. Never could, and thought I never would. I tried for a good part of my life, and always came up short.

Thankfully this inability to forgive others was merely a stopping point along the road to another, even more important, realization.

My forgiveness challenge was transformed when I took a good long look at the Aramaic meanings of "forgive." I was reviewing my translation, from the King James Lord's Prayer back into an Aramaic form, which used the list of word meanings found in The Hidden Gospel, Decoding the Spiritual Message of the Aramaic Jesus by Neil Douglas-Klotz.

"And forgive us our trespasses as we forgive those who trespass against us." (King James Lord's Prayer)

"Set us free from our errors and frustrated hopes, as we seek to set free those who are in error against us."(An Aramaic Lord's Prayer; my translation using Aramaic word meanings of the KJLP words)

"Set free," found in the second sentence of my Aramaic translation, is an alternate meaning for the Aramaic "sebaq" (forgive). Other meanings include: "To restore to its original state: loosen, let go, set free, omit." I also checked out Love Forgiveness.com. There, sebaq meanings included "to cancel, loosen or untie." My two favorites were "untie" and "set free." I have a profound appreciation for personal autonomy. So any attitude that "unties" and "sets free" personal choice, and thus offers autonomy, is a magnet to my interest. Sebaq qualifies.

In my mind up popped two questions: How is sebaq to be applied to my daily living, which is riddled with behavioral errors, shortcomings, unwanted surprises and losses? And how can sebaq be applied to dissolve my anger, sadness, anxiety, and disgust? When I reflect on these two questions, a list of life lessons and two of my life experiences come to mind.

Life lessons:

I may not be able to forgive others, but I can choose to untie myself from their behavior through my own self talk, my own empathic understanding, and my own reframing of the troubling behavior.

The "sebaqness" may include any of the following realms: physical, mental, emotional, spiritual (attitudinal).

When I choose to "sebaq", and to the degree I do so, I can be more free to observe effectively. I can be more free in choosing how to dissolve threat without using punishment. I can be more free to use my creative imagination. I can be more free to respond effectively and empathically to unreasonable demands. I can choose to honor myself, and thus be less susceptible to shame. I can increase my capacity to embrace personal responsibility. I can reduce my psychic pain from negative emotions. I can enjoy an increased sense of autonomy and its accompanying self-esteem. I can embrace an ethics of feelings and needs, beyond moralistic good-bad   ethics. I can feel bodily relaxation seep into the areas of my body where I hold tension.

Graduate School Experience:

Forgiveness played an important role in my early career efforts. In the 1990's I was in the last phase of my grad school psychology studies. I had landed one of the rare psych internships, mine being a nine-month mental health counseling position at an inner city clinic. My grad school supplied two psychologist-supervisors. One was a 75-year-old seasoned veteran of the field, whose only shortcoming was to occasionally doze off in our weekly 1:1 supervisories. My other supervisor was a Ph.D. in her mid-fifties, who never smiled. Without an understanding as to why, soon I realized I was in deep supervisory trouble. In her presence my memory kept flashing on the Wicked Witch of the West. For the first eight months she squeezed every drop of forgiveness I could generate to titrate her toxic criticisms. During the weekly group and 1:1 supervisions, I remember repeatedly saying to myself, "I forgive this woman. I forgive this woman. I forgive this woman." By the seventh month I was seeing a psychologist to reduce my unbearable anxiety.

My classmates confided in me that they had advised her that I was really "a good guy and competent," and suggested that she lighten up on me. She didn't. Until the ninth month, when suddenly I was ok. She wrote a final evaluation listing my strengths and including a strong recommendation that I had satisfied all the competencies required by the internship. I had the report mounted in a $110 black walnut frame, and hung it on the wall just over our master bedroom toilet. The new wall decor was good for daily smiles. It was a reminder of the social, and personal, power of forgiveness. After all, forgiveness had played a critical role in facilitating my internship success and my graduation.

I found out a couple months later that she was going through a nasty divorce, and I looked just like her husband.

Trumpet Performance Experience:

My second use of sebaq occurred just after a remarkable orchestral trumpet performance.

One day before a Santa Barbara Symphony concert I was told that the Principal Trumpet was sick and that I was to take his place. There would be no orchestra rehearsal. I arranged for a last-minute sectional rehearsal with the other two trumpet players.

The concert included the Second Symphony of Jean Sibelius. Sibelius loved the expressive sound of the trumpet, and used it generously in his symphonic orchestrations. Waves of sonorous brass passion.

The trumpet section nailed it. Total precision. Total risk-laden orchestral trumpet performance. Just after the magnificent final chord, and just before the applause and bravos, Ernie the second-chair trumpet player, bent over close to me and said,"That's the worst goddamned trumpet playing I've ever heard." His comment was about my playing, as was obvious from the angry look on his face. A bucket of icewater over a principal trumpet player, transitioning from the white-hot focus of peak performance.

          SNIPPETS of a GRANDFATHER'S LIFE

Luckily for both of us I had been introduced recently to a process of interpersonal communication that was designed to deal with such an emotionally violent scenario (Marshall Rosenberg's Nonviolent Communication). Immediately I recognized this situation as a sparkling opportunity to apply my newly acquired Nonviolent Communication skills. I applied the process which required setting my needs aside for the moment, and thus being freed to begin generating empathy for Ernie's experience.

"So Ernie, please tell me what about my playing tonight prompted your anger? I'm all ears."

Thus went the communication until I noticed that we were the only two musicians remaining on the stage. With the tension being reduced, both his eyes and mine began to smile. Sebaq had made its appearance.

Ernie left the stage laughing to himself. I asked him why he was laughing. He said,"It was your response." A month later I found out Ernie had a brain tumor.

My conclusions: Sebaq is a keeper…as long as my goal and process is to sebaq (untie) myself from the unwanted behavior of others. I can't untie others from their behaviors, nor can I fathom the complexity driving others to do what they do. I can only untie myself.

One of the fundamental principles of human performance is that error always exists within excellent performance. Error can be quite small; however, it is always there. There is another performance process where error is always found. It is present within the brain as an essential part of learning.

Professor Thad A. Polk (The Great Courses, "The Addictive Brain," Lecture 2) discusses the Rescorla-Wagner model of learning, which says that we learn through prediction error. In other words, we do not change our response to stimuli as long as our predictions of outcomes are accurate. We change when our predictions are inaccurate. We LEARN when our predictions are inaccurate.

Because the lecture is about addiction, Polk discusses the areas of the brain involved in pleasure. The three areas are the nucleus accumbens (the seat of pleasure), the prefrontal cortex (the region which controls behavior, sets goals, and makes sure that the goals are accomplished), and the ventral tegmental area, VTA (the primitive area that signals both the nucleus accumbens and the prefrontal cortex).

The VTA fires off its signal neurotransmitter (dopamine) when a prediction error is made, thus pleasure-based learning is initiated. In other words, WE LEARN BY MAKING ERRORS.

We learn by making emotionally painful prediction errors as well. The following is a vignette which illustrates such an error.

Sitting in the first-row audience seat, my trumpet student saw it coming. I didn't. In symphonic trumpet parlance a mistake, or wrong note, is called a "clam." My American Heritage Dictionary of the English Language gives some clue to the term's derivation in its entry for the word clamor: "to make a loud sustained noise."

That evening the chamber orchestra, choir and I with my piccolo trumpet in hand, performed Magnificat by Johann Sebastian Bach. The principal trumpet part has a dominant role in the fabric of this baroque masterpiece. Bach wrote it to feature the upper register of the instrument. The entrances are "forte," which means strong. When a trumpet player sees "forte" on the page, it can mean STRONG.

The piccolo trumpet is pitched a full octave above a regular trumpet and it is the smallest instrument in the symphonic trumpeter's tool kit. Mine has four valves, three of which are used to play its normal range. That means that finger tips are aligned with valves 1, 2 and 3. The fourth valve, which is located closest to the bell, is occasionally used to extend the low end of the instrument's pitch range.

Because of the tiny size of the instrument, the valves are only a few inches from the player's nose. That evening, on one of my forte (STRONG) entrances, my fingers mistakenly lined up on valves 2, 3 and 4. It is safe to say that Bach did not write what came smashing out of that trumpet. It was a clam. It was not an ordinary run-of-the-mill clam. It was one of those National Geographic Magazine South Pacific giant clams.

Flabbergasted, I ripped the trumpet from my lips, flipped the horn around, and peered down the bell, expecting to see some foreign object plugging the tubing. No foreign object. Momentarily confused, I instinctively found my way back into the music, performing flawlessly for the remainder of the performance.

My confusion was relieved when the student rushed up after the concert and told me what I had done. He said he had noticed my misplaced fingers, saw the clam coming, and felt an immediate sense of helpless dread. He cringed at the clam, as did everyone else. There are no hiding places in trumpet performance.

I know that surprise (from prediction error) is the emotion associated with the process of learning. Surprise is not an adequate word to describe the branding-iron lesson the magnificent clam taught me. You can bet that my brain's emotional memory prompts me to double-check my finger placement every time I raise my piccolo trumpet in a concert.

That concert took place forty years ago.

For twenty-three years, as Principal Trumpet of a major German orchestra, my new client had suffered from excess performance anxiety (stage fright). He said he had tried several psychotherapies, without success. He wanted to be introduced to Masterful Life-Performance, the approach to performance put forth in my book, ON CUE, Managing Anxiety, Inviting Excellence. He and I spent five hours, by phone from Germany. We covered all the basics of ML-P, one of which is that performance anxiety can be reduced by believing that our performance is a gift when we perform FOR others.

He was acutely interested in the effects of the increase of Social Interest on one's concert performance. Social Interest (Gemeinschaftsgefuehl) is found in the social psychology of Alfred Adler. It refers to one's sense of social connectedness to community and intent to contribute to the commonweal. I prefer a simple interpretation of the concept. I think of Social Interest as the intent to GIVE TO the audience, rather than GET FROM the audience. One of the statistical conclusions of my research is that performers with the intent to give the gift of their performance experience less stage fright than those who hold the intent to get from the audience.

He came up with his own ingenious stage fright reduction strategy, based on Social Interest. He imagined that his best trumpet student was sitting beside him in the concert, and he was showing the student how the part was to be played. He was GIVING a trumpet lesson during the concert.

He gave me two follow-up reports. The first said that he had experienced the most relaxed concert that he could remember. The second was that he had experienced the best season of his career.

I have a confession to make. It's not easy for a proud man like myself to make confessions. Even though we know on some level that our uniqueness is on par with everyone else's uniqueness. Still, revealing certain behaviors is unnerving. There's a real risk here.

Some of my liberal-thinking friends would call it self-care. Others would be surprised. They would think of me differently.

The behavior takes fifteen minutes. I'm very good at it. I've done it for a long time. I do it at the same time, only once, every week. On Wednesday afternoon between 1:10 and 1:25 I have a break between psychotherapy client sessions. It's the release that I look forward to. There's something about the ritual that allows me to suspend self-judgment. Upon reflection, it's not always rewarding, but rewards with enough consistency so that I feel compelled to do it again.

There's a certain place where I do it. Every town of any size has such a place. Pretty much everybody is aware of these establishments. They're usually not in the best part of town. The one I go to has a back parking lot, which I use because it is important that I get in and out quickly.

Last Wednesday I did it again. I slipped through the back door.

For me, entering into Lenny's Discount Clothing Outlet is similar to entering a church sanctuary. I can leave all my cares at the door. I can concentrate on the possibility that I might, just might, have an epiphany shopping experience.

You guessed it. Last Wednesday it happened big time. There, hanging on the closeout winter coat rack was a magnificently designed Irish loden green wool coat. Simple panels of thick woolen fabric, carefully stitched. The zipper looked like it would last 100 years. I'd never seen such a sturdy, yet elegant, masculine design in a winter coat. And it was my size, 42 chest.

I checked the price. No price tag.

It was paired on the same hanger with the largest pair of gray woolen trousers I'd ever seen. I thought of my friend Friedeman Immer, the famous German baroque trumpeter. Friedeman is seven foot one. Those pants would fit him just fine. The price tag on the pants read $65. I motioned to the salesclerk and I asked what the price was for the coat. She said the two were a pair and the price was $65 for both items.

I told her of my interest in the coat only, and said I'd be pleased to split the price and buy just the coat. She thought for a moment, and said she'd take $40 for the coat. I may have ripped my back pocket a little getting my wallet out. As she put the coat in a large plastic Lenny's shopping bag, I noticed small carefully embroidered lettering on the top back of the garment. It read "Stormy Kromer 1903."

When I got home, I Googled Stormy Kromer, and checked out the price of their Mackinaw Coat. It was $289.

I confess. I ripped off Lenny's.

I seek:

An Earth free of war and the threat of war.

I seek:

A society with equity and justice for all.

I seek:

A community where every person's potential may be fulfilled.

I seek:

An Earth restored.

I seek:

A humanity that chooses a loving Vision of Divinity as its Ultimate and Ideal Interior Audience.

MISSION STATEMENT

As long as I live, I commit all my resources to maximizing my effectiveness as co-creator with and within my Vision of Divinity, and co-creator with and within the lives of others, for improving the quality of living for others and for myself, with special attention to those whom I hold most dear, and extending to all sentient life on Earth. My intent is to do this by striving to be alert and receptive to truth, in all its forms, settings, systems, and presenting circumstances. It is also my intent to invite my Vision of Divinity to be my constant unconditionally encouraging Internal Audience and Source of Internal Direction, by which and through which my Creative Performing Self is empowered to work, learn, rest and play in the predominant mood of calm gladness, and within the attitudinal constellation of unconditional acceptance, forgiveness, trust, empathy, humor, presence and gratitude.

For an orchestral trumpeter, performing a High D in concert demands an all-out effort, a nothing held back, a 100% go-for-it attitude. When it is accompanied by a sign indicating "FF" (double forte), it means to go for it "double strong" (LOUD).

In six chamber orchestra rehearsals and two concerts, that is exactly what I did. I gave it my all, all my trumpet expertise, all my physical strength, and all my emotional courage. One might say my High D's mowed down any other orchestra sounds present. The trumpet timbre dominated like a ballet-dancing bull in the proverbial china shop, exactly as the composer, Benjamin Britten, had indicated.

At the second rehearsal I noticed that the violinists sitting in front of me had moved, out of harm's way.

I nailed the High D in six rehearsals and the first concert. At the second concert I changed my eyeglasses for better focus. I also adjusted the music stand to be a bit closer. That was all well and good; however, in reaction to the emotional intensity of the High D entrance, I placed the trumpet bell too close to the music stand. When I attacked (and it is called an attack) the D with full force, the reverberation off the stand returned a sound wave that rendered my High D a third of a tone flat. My musical instincts immediately took over in an attempt to raise the pitch. This caused the tone to oscillate into an upper overtone. Suffice to say, for a split-second it was an ugly dissonant mess. My musical instincts still in crisis mode, I immediately and momentarily stopped playing.

Trumpeters have a label for such a mistake. It is called a "Clam." It has been reported that the Principal Trumpet of a major American orchestra has "CLAM" on his license plate. I'm seriously thinking about doing this as well.

My High D clam was an emotionally violent surprise to me and to those poor musicians close by. I liken it to throwing a bucket of ice water on a climaxing orchestra. The music was unfamiliar and modern, so the audience probably thought my clam was written in the part.

Appreciating the rest of an otherwise excellent performance, during the applause, the conductor waved to me to stand to take a bow. I was sufficiently rumpled to ignore her wave. I didn't stand. I hadn't entered the resilience stage of emotional recovery.

After the concert, just as I entered the backstage musicians' room, I inadvertently overheard a conversation between the timpanist and the conductor. They were discussing a clam that the timpanist had made in another piece. She empathized with him. "It's all history to me."

Then the timpanist shared with her his newly acquired performance attitude that had made a significant positive contribution to reducing his performance anxiety and adding to his joy. He told her of how he used the attitude of forgiveness to "untie himself" from the negativity of his performance error. It was a breath of fresh insight that he had recently learned from reading a book on the subject (ON CUE, Managing Anxiety Inviting Excellence). He told her it was a good read, and recommended it to her.

He was talking about my book. I quietly thanked the Universe for another instructive performance lesson. So much about performance is learning to respond constructively to an error. That evening, I reread ON CUE.

I expect that you are familiar with lust. Most people are. My object of lust does not take on the usual and normal forms. Sex, drugs, gambling, alcohol, violence, social power-domination hold little fascination for me. Mine has taken on the form of an automobile. To be specific, a 2002 black Jaguar XKR convertible. The XKR is a supercharged version of the XK8, which is a descendent of the XKE, an automobile that is widely understood to be the most beautiful sports car ever created.

My fascination with Jaguars began with a fire engine red 1962 XKE coupe that I bought from a guy who loved to work on XKE's. He would do a total restoration including paint, and sell them for the price of the materials he had put into the restoration. I bought number six for $1,500.

The high point of my ownership of this car involved a short stretch of paved road connecting Santa Barbara to its neighboring community of Goleta. In the mid 70's that one-mile stretch was undeveloped. No houses, no strip-malls, no highway patrolmen. As the motor went from purr to roar the whole rest of the car quieted down. It was as if it was remembering its racecar pedigree. The speedometer read 90… and I was only in second.

My next Jaguar was a 1986 British racing green SJ6. A drop-dead gorgeous sedan. As I drove off the used-car lot I reached up to adjust the rearview mirror. It came off in my hand. If I had been smart, I would have driven back to the used car lot, parked it, and walked away. I would have been money ahead.

Early in this ownership adventure, I noticed that the tires seemed a bit small. I checked the manual, and sure enough, a larger size was indicated. I changed them out. Within a half a mile three out of the four were shredded. The car had been in an accident and the frame was diagonally out of specs. The smaller tires went back on. Shortly after that I read in the Santa Barbara Newspress that the owner of the used car lot had gone to prison. Income tax evasion or something.

On the final day of ownership, while driving the back roads to work I smelled gas. I stopped and opened the hood. Gas was spewing out a broken gas line onto a hot engine. I decided that this goddamned car was going to kill me. That day I bought a Volvo sedan. It was one of the best cars that I have ever owned.

But back to the shiny 2002 XKR convertible. For the last three months one of these, a beautifully conditioned low-mileage one, has been hanging out at a local dealer's lot. It has beckoned me like the flittering eyelids of a gorgeous beauty. I deny any sexual overtones. My wife, Maggie, says, "Think again."

I noticed a distinct mixture of sadness and emotional relief when it disappeared off the lot this week. My wallet seemed to grow a bit thicker, as if it had taken a deep breath and escaped a serious threat.

A while back I thought it would be interesting and instructive to write down the half-dozen or so life lessons my father, Ronald Hepworth Thompson, taught me. Few of the resulting listings were spoken, as he taught primarily by example.

"Be gentle with your lover." (Birds and Bees conversation)

Be honest, especially with yourself.

Avoid conceit.

Avoid prejudice.

Avoid presumptuousness.

Avoid self-pity.

Embrace learning and knowledge.

Honor honest accomplishment.

"Give the other guy the benefit of the doubt."

Avoid boastfulness.

Honor and respect "Mother Nature."

"Avoid counting your chickens before they hatch."

Value partial solutions.

"Half a pee is better than none at all."

Value your friendships.

Be helpful to your friends.

Be supportive to your family.

"Set your own house in order first."

Avoid greediness.

Avoid being fussy about your clothing.

Be thrifty.

Embrace self-control.

Save up, then buy.

Watch for a good deal.

Avoid being in debt.

Be inventive.

Understand how things work.

Think smart. Act smart.

Be thoughtful.

Think before you speak.

Talk about issues and conditions, not people.

Avoid gossip.

Avoid talking about yourself.

Trust yourself first.

Trust your intellect before your emotions.

Be monogamous.

Be adventuresome.

Plan ahead.

"Don't go to bed with anybody you don't want to spend the rest of your life with."

Be self-accepting.

Take calculated risks.

Honor knowledge.

Honor and pursue education.

Be private.

"Don't share your dirty laundry with anybody."

Be industrious.

Enjoy sex with your life partner.

Enjoy clever humor.

Don't hire someone else to do what you can learn to do yourself.

Keep your tools in great working order.

Include friends.

Honor all ethical people regardless of age, gender, race, nationality, sexual orientation, economic status, physical condition, or educational status.

Have a clear understanding about the difference between necessities and luxuries.

Waste not, want not.

"You can lead a horse to water…"

Enjoy the out-of-doors.

"Mother Nature" is bounteous.

Finish what you start.

"Accomplishing anything of value isn't easy."

Avoid fearfulness.

Honor courage.

"Take the time to do it right the first time."

Be curious.

Follow your interests.

Be an independent thinker.

Take your time.

Be open-minded.

Balance work and recreation.

Be kind.

Be realistic.

Be generous, but not to a fault.

Be calm and interested.

Trust life.

Be content.

Aesthetics is important.

Honor mental hygiene.

Take responsibility for your mind.

Take responsibility for your behavior.

Take responsibility for your sexuality.

Own up to your errors. "Face the music."

Think inside and outside the box.

Be fully accepting of circumstance.

Notice patterns in Nature, especially human nature.

Seek excellence in craftsmanship.

Look at the big picture.

Enjoy corny humor.

Do the best you can with what you've got.

Play for keeps. And don't be afraid of giving some of it away.

Let the extent of your cursing be "damn!"

Don't trust clergy or psychologists.*

*Please note that I spent two years studying theology at Bloy House Episcopal Seminary, and have been a Licensed Psychologist Master for over 29 years. Dad's ancestry is littered with celebrated clergy. What a hoot!

Dad Giving a Presentation

　　　SNIPPETS of a GRANDFATHER'S LIFE

Ronald "Tommy" Thompson

When I asked my daughter Betsy how she liked her freshly baked, four-layer coconut white cake with vanilla cream cheese frosting, she said it "wasn't bad."

I need to explain what she meant, because I tasted it and judged it to be the best white cake I had ever eaten. I would not use the descriptor "not bad." Immediately, I translated her evaluation into Californian. Having spent forty-two years of my life in California I pronounced it Terrific! Great! Amazing! Best I'd ever eaten! I promptly helped myself to a rather generous second piece.

You see, Betsy spent eight years of her childhood in Minnesota. In Minnesota "not bad" really means "excellent." It might even mean "Great." However, you wouldn't catch a Minnesotan boasting about anything, including great cake.

Her mother, Maggie, had a piece too. She said, "Boy, is that wonderful cake!" She spent her childhood on an Illinois dairy farm.

All of us were describing the same cake. Betsy and I at the two extremes of social appropriateness and Maggie smack dab in the center. That's how it goes in our house.

There's something that has disturbed me for a long time (actually for years). Plain and simple, it's the news, or more precisely the degree of negative and disturbing content of the news. As I puzzled over my relationship with the news and other social media, I have realized that this relationship is one of love and disgust. I love knowing what's going on, being informed. I feel disgust when I experience how negative events and the underbelly of society, my society, are over reported.

While reading a book on the neurology of sleep (The Secret World of Sleep, by Penelope A. Lewis), I was finally able to assemble an explanation of how I could untie myself from my disgust with the media, and thus forge a more emotionally healthy path ahead. While writing about dreaming, Ms. Lewis reported that it is easier for the human brain to remember negative events than positive ones. This simple fact led me to the hypothesis that our attention to negative events is a survival behavior. We pay attention to that which threatens us. That which is going just fine can be ignored. On a social scale the news and other social media are our way of paying attention to that which threatens us. The role of media is therefore valuable and necessary.

My challenge is to absorb the valuable truth that social media has to offer, and maintain a healthy perspective while doing so. Through my study of psychology, I have learned that the emotion of calm gladness is the emotion most associated with emotional health. My challenge is to embrace social media and maintain, and even increase, calm gladness. In order to do that I have accepted the obvious fact, obvious at least to me, that the reality of my world is far more complex than social media is able to report. Far more complex. Infinitely more complex. Within that complexity there exists a degree of goodness and loving functionality that goes largely unnoticed. My belief is that it is both our attention to threat and our living in an ocean of loving functionality that has resulted in our survival as a species for eons.

Albert Einstein said that the most important question we can ask is if the Universe is a friendly place. I believe that my daily dose of news and social media misses almost all the friendliness of the Universe and, even with its severe shortcomings, supplies valuable information. This belief goes a long way to forging a perspective which allows me to remain emotionally strong, even when the news is bad.

Her body moved with the grace and poise of a professional dancer, which she had been. Her passion for dance and love of children led her to become the dance teacher of generations of kids in Geneva, Illinois. Expressive beyond expressive, even the casual encounter with Edith involved her arms outstretched, ready for the all-embarrassing hug, and the genuine inquiry as to how you were doing. Kids were known to cross State Street in the middle of the block to avoid being part of this spectacle. "Oh-oh, look, she's coming our way." She was the perfect Bloody Mary in Geneva's production of South Pacific.

For decades Edith Gibson taught "Fortnightly", where the white-gloved boys and girls were instructed in the social graces. The foxtrot, the waltz, and the rumba were among the basics. Modern Dance classes were offered to the girls only.

When my wife Maggie's mother was stricken with cancer, it was Edith who drove Ethel so many times the forty miles to and from her Chicago oncologist. When Maggie was called back from boarding school because of the untimely death of her beloved father, it was Edith who met the young grieving Maggie at O'Hare Airport.

The day Maggie's handwritten letter to Edith was returned unopened, and the short phone call to her care facility verified Edith's passing, was a day of sadness in our home. It was not the desolate sadness of bereavement. It was a sadness tempered by the joy of our having known a truly loving human being.

We sat around the dinner table throwing out names for the soft gold, sleek-bodied Jaguar XK8 coupe I had just bought. Maggie's Nissan Rogue was "Ethel," named for her mom. Daughter Betsy's Nissan "Earl," for Maggie's father. Daughter Sylvia's Honda CRV, "Zorro." He's shiny black. My Honda CRV, "My Car." Lack of creativity here.

"She would love that!" Maggie was emphatic when I suggested the Jaguar be named "Edith Gibson." Considering elegance and expressiveness, it was the name that matched human being with automobile.

I wholeheartedly agreed with Maggie. "Edith would be tickled. I can see her expressive eyes open wide, and her hands reaching to the sky."

"Why you daaarlings…thank you for thinking of me!"

2021 CHAPIN ROAD, CALAIS VERMONT

There she was lying in the weeds beside the dirt road which bordered my farm and my neighbor's pasture. She was a 1940's floor lamp, nestled there like a sleeping fairy tale princess, crowned with the gaudiest pink lampshade imaginable. I felt compelled to hesitate on my morning walk and set her back upright against the old fencepost. It was the least I could do to acknowledge her unique royalty.

But how in heaven's name had she landed there? What chain of circumstances had transpired? As I continued my morning walk, with the quiet forest my only companion, my curiosity cycled in an effort to connect the memory dots. Let's see. There had been an old pickup truck rusting in the pasture close by. It was gone. I thought I'd caught sight of it on a junker's trailer as it passed by me the other day on Route 14. That must be it. The lamp was part of the load of scrap metal. It must have fallen out as the trailer load bounced onto Chapin. Explanation enough.

But now, what to do about her? Such a unique opportunity, and she's so cute. Out of place like a Capezio dance slipper resting next to a barn door. I just have to get her lighted up.

Aubuchon Hardware had a vast array of solar driveway lights. I bought the brightest one they had, 5 lumens, eight bucks. After a couple tries with some baling wire, I fastened it in, all four miniature solar LED lights hidden just inside the pink lampshade. Voila! Now the wait until the night darkness.

No light emanated from her that evening. It was time to go home and read the directions.

After turning the ON switch to ON, I let her charge in the sunlight all the next day. That night she glowed just like she belonged there.

On my walk the next day, I asked a couple neighbors who live on the road if they had noticed anything unusual coming home from work after dark. Big smiles and the same chorus: "So that was you!" One neighbor promised to "keep the snow off her come winter."

Chapin Road Utility

The other day I realized that I like to exercise my imagination. Not the kind of imagining that erodes the quality of life, but the kind that enhances it, like how brightly colored ornaments bring to life a Christmas tree. That's why I like to write creative nonfiction. Its cloth is laced with the threads of imagination and imperfect memory. I use this writing form to deliver what I believe to be greater truths.

One of the favorite imaginings is that I tell myself I know something about God. The naked truth is that I don't, but that doesn't keep me from thinking theological thoughts, especially when they have the effect of quieting my mind.

If I start with acknowledging my profound ignorance of God, I can move on to something of greater pragmatism. My personal theology, as lived out in daily life, is what counts. It is a prism through which I interpret the events of life.

Recently, I noticed in my trumpet performance journal that I am within 100 performances of a life total of 4,000. It's no wonder I use "performance" as a metaphor for my behavior. Using that metaphor, I hold the belief that life is primarily performed from the inside out. So, it's a small step to my Vision of God as my Ultimate Interior Audience.

Implicit in performance is the presence of audience, whether we are aware of that presence or not. I believe Carl Jung, the often-quoted Viennese psychologist, would agree. His tombstone reads: "BIDDEN OR NOT BIDDEN GOD IS PRESENT."

Here's where my imagination, my life experience and Jung's theology intersect. I've noticed that there is a positive correlation between the ease and beauty of my trumpet performance and the presence of a loving Ultimate Interior Audience to which I choose to perform.

Bidden

A long time ago somebody said to me, "You can't live in a sewer and come out smelling like a rose." I believe there's merit to this bit of wisdom, in that the context of our lives is a primary determiner of the way by which we interpret communication coming from others.

In my work with angry adolescents, I often hear the "F" word. If the rage is strong enough and the vocabulary sufficiently underdeveloped, every other word qualifies. That's all well and good when it comes from the mouth of a raging teen, but when it comes from the mouth of a priest and is directed at me, it leaves me immediately hyper-vigilant and confused.

This morning as I was sitting in a pew with my trumpet in hand, waiting for the choir director to rehearse the hymn on which I play a trumpet descant, the priest silently mouthed the "F" word in my direction. I was instantly on guard. How could this guy be so crass towards me? I attend regularly. I am up-to-date with my pledge. I support my cradle-Episcopalian wife in her deep appreciation of, and significant contribution to, the church. I joyfully donate my trumpet expertise Sunday morning after Sunday morning.

He mouthed it twice more, each time with increasing vehemence. Finally, he said it out loud.

HAPPY FATHER'S DAY!

Anonymous:

"Because I have been athirst, I will dig a well that others may drink."

"Reading can seriously damage your ignorance."

Martha Beck:

"Love is the only thing on this earth that lets us see each other with the remotest accuracy."

Nancy Beck:

"Positive attitude is everything. I have seen many people think themselves well."

Gautama Buddha:

"You yourself, as much as anybody in the entire Universe, deserve your love and affection". (The Moto Calendar, PO Box 1383, Pottstown, PA 19464-1383)

Note: I would change the word "deserve" to "need."

"You will not be punished for your anger. You will be punished by your anger."

Marcus Tullius Cicero:

"Gratitude is not only the greatest of virtues, but the parent of all others."

Cyril Connolly:

"Better to write for yourself and have no public than to write for the public and have no self."

Dutch Wisdom:

Neit geschoten altyd mis.

If you don't shoot, you miss.

Meister Eckhart:

"If the only prayer you ever say is thank you, that would suffice."

Albert Einstein:

"Creativity is intelligence having fun."

"I never teach my pupils. I only provide the conditions in which they can learn."

"The single most important decision any of us will have to make is whether or not to believe the Universe is friendly."

Ralph Waldo Emerson:

"The measure of mental health is the disposition to find good everywhere."

Fortune Cookie Wisdom:

"Fear is just excitement in need of an attitude adjustment."

Patricia Fontaine:

"It is clear and basic kindness that we can offer ourselves, and becoming familiar with it, offer it to others."

Christopher Fry:

"What she gave to us in life we hold in trust, not to be diminished by her dying   but to make greater room in ourselves to contain what she gave; to make memory work for its living, and to make the bare place of absence fertile."

Jane Galbraith:

"A book can really make a difference."

Johann Wolfgang von Goethe:

"The way you see people is the way you treat them, and the way you treat them is the way they become."

Stephen Hawking:

"One of the basic rules of the universe is that NOTHING IS PERFECT. Perfection simply doesn't exist… without imperfection, neither you nor I would exist."

William James:

"The greatest revolution of our generation is the discovery that human beings, by changing the inner attitudes of their minds, can change the outer aspects of their lives."

James Joyce:

"Mistakes are the portals of discovery."

Carl Jung:

"Bidden or not bidden God is present."

"The reality of the psyche is the primary reality."

The Lord's Prayer: King James Bible

Our Father, who art in heaven, hallowed be thy name. Thy kingdom come. Thy will be done, as it is in heaven. Give us this day our daily bread. And forgive us our trespasses as we forgive those who trespass against us. Lead us not into temptation but deliver us from evil. For thine is the kingdom and the power and the glory, forever and ever. Amen.

The Lord's Prayer: As reverse-translated from the King James to an Aramaic version by R.E.Thompson:

Our Creator, who exists in the place of light without limit, whose light is the pivot point upon which all of creation turns, and whose ruling vision, consent, and joy arises in nature even as a host of stars brings its unlimited brilliance to the firmament. Give to us this day our daily empathic understanding. Untie us from our errors and frustrated hopes, as we seek to untie those who are in error against us. Counsel us so as to avoid that which would tempt us to be out of rhythm with your vision for us. For your counsel and guidance are empowerment and pure delight, now and forever. Amen.

Anne Lamott: American

"Laughter is carbonated holiness."

Pablo Picasso:

"The meaning of life is to find your gift. The purpose of life is to give it away."

Mstislav Rostropovich:

"The artist must forget the audience, forget the critics, forget the technique, forget everything but love for the music. Then, the music speaks through the performance, and the performer and the listener will walk together with the soul of the composer, and with God."

Jelaluddin Rumi:

"For sixty years I have been forgetful every moment,

but not for a second has this flowing toward me stopped or slowed. I deserve nothing. Today I recognize that I am the guest the mystics talk about. I play this living music for my Host. Everything today is for the Host.”

“Out beyond ideas of wrong-doing and right-doing there is a field. I’ll meet you there.”

“Then new events said to me, don’t move. A sublime generosity is coming toward you.”

“It makes absolutely no difference what people think of you.”

“Gamble everything for love, if you are a true human being. If not, leave this gathering. Half-heartedness doesn’t reach into majesty. You set out to find God, but then you keep stopping for long periods at mean-spirited roadhouses.”

Plutarch:

“What we achieve inwardly will change outer reality.”

R.E.Thompson:

“Ah. The sweetness of feeling outside of time.”

“Anger is little more than an emotional pain deflector, a deflector of sadness due to past loss and/or anxiety due to projected future loss.”

“Completing a life-affirming task which requires delayed self-gratification is a source of calm-gladness. Eating really good blue cheese is another.”

"It's easy if I apply the level of gratitude necessary to break it down into small enough steps."

"We're all flying toward the same runway."

"Generally, accomplishment is simple, and not necessarily easy".

"Art is the expression of hidden intelligence."

"In large measure, circumstance chooses my outer audience. I choose my inner audience."

"If you believe that a manifestation of the presence of God is unconditionally loving attitude, what roadmap for choice in personal attitude does that belief imply?"

"Gratitude expressed completes the cycle of creativity and invites movement toward the territory ahead."

"Invariably, I see a path."

"I have met my responsibilities. Now I drink tea."

"I think the world has no need of armies, and has need of a million more orchestras. Maybe ten million more."

"I think people who talk as if they know all about God, don't. I believe they know what they believe about the nature of God, and may know that quite thoroughly, and demonstrate that by living out their beliefs."

"It pays off to smell good."

"There's an internal payoff for doing social-contributory work and striving to do it in an excellent manner. The "internal" is my point."

"It's love that keeps us alive."

"Fear of God is an oxymoron."

"Oh, that life would always present to us circumstance to which we have the ethical reserve to respond with loving attitude."

"Most of the time I never lie."

"God is love. Present, bidden or not bidden." To be carved on my tombstone, or my funeral urn.

"Orchestral trumpet performance has the social exposure intensity of a first visit to a nudist colony."

"Self is the most reliable and available source of encouragement."

"The idea is to create a lifestyle that maximizes creative choice and minimizes harmful dependencies."

"The job of the performer is to create the gift and deliver it." And "That's all folks." (Thanks be to Bugs Bunny.)

"The goal of the Perfectionist is to create perfect performance by beating himself/herself into perfection. In the Universe perfection does not exist, therefore the Perfectionist just ends up emotionally beaten, and with reduced productivity."

"The goal of the Excellist is to create excellent performance by loving himself/herself into excellence. In the Universe excellence is everywhere, and the Excellest ends up emotionally healthy and productive."

"There's no such thing as entitlement."

"There's plenty of room at the top if one is open-minded as to the meaning of top."

"Music performance can be the frosting on the cake of life."

"Loving truth is my sanctuary."

"One of the best reasons in the world is: Because I choose to."

"The primary virtue that has resulted in my living into my advanced age is my willingness to risk making an error. Other than that, I'm lucky as hell."

"No gratitude, no empowerment."

"No trust, no forward movement."

"The Rescorla-Wagner Model explains that the human brain learns through prediction error. Is it not freeing to think that the primary way in which we learn is through making errors, making mistakes? Ah, the blessed screwup."

"I play for keeps, then give it away. Incorporating this into my lifestyle leads me to experience both accomplishment and meaning."

"I am spiritually connected to my Vision of God when I choose to respond to life circumstance with loving attitude."

"I nibble away at my challenges, until they vanish. It's just like eating cold Brussels sprouts."

"It is essential for one's emotional and physical health, to carve out of the Chaos one's own concept of the Divine, and live so as to be in rhythm with it."

"I can tell when my lifestyle is working. It is when I carry loving attitudes towards myself and others. When I accidentally drop my car keys in the snow, and smile."

"I continue to do trumpet performance so that I will not lose touch with the challenges my stagefright clients face."

"Divinity is Love, and is revealed in Creation in a myriad of ways, loving attitude being the most common and helpful to human experience. My invitation to myself is to get with the program."

"My process is to create a lifestyle from which I do not crave a vacation."

"The Universe has provided me with everything I have ever wanted, times 1000, or maybe 10,000. Perhaps not as quickly as I would have preferred, but make no mistake, everything I have ever wanted."

"My primary spiritual discipline is to collect self-generated thoughts of gratitude each day. No, each hour. No, each minute."

"Playing trumpet out of tune and not knowing it is like having bad breath".

"There will be times when the desire to perform will be at ebbtide."

"The most functional I can Be is to focus my consciousness on choosing Gratitude as my primary life attitude, thus remain connected to my Vision of God, and enjoy the ride to the maximum I am capable."

"The best way to prepare for death is to choose a life well-lived."

"This delayed-gratification stuff gets old."

"The first step in anger management is to acknowledge the presence of anger. The second is to be aware of the sadness (as prompted by past loss) or anxiety (prompted by the anticipation of future loss) that drives the anger. The third is to understand what specific personal loss, or projected loss, prompts the sadness or anxiety. The fourth is to create a non-violent compassionate strategy to address the unmet need associated with the identified loss, thus initiating the reduction of painful emotion. The fifth is to execute the strategy. The sixth is to express gratitude for the outcome of the effort. The seventh is to return to the first step with a measure of self-created calm gladness, thus moving from strength to strength."

"Calm gladness is about as pleasant as it gets."

"My sense of choice is as close to a definition of my "Soul" as has ever come to me."

"Today will bring wonderful opportunities to respond lovingly to social-emotional challenges."

"A sin is nothing more or less than error, a missing of the mark. It is an ancient archery term. I believe, when I sufficiently learn the lessons embedded in my sins, my errors, the learning increases the likelihood I will be a bit more fully human."

The Music Empowers Foundation:

"Music is my connection to what the world doesn't know about me."

Unknown:

"The quiet mind is richer than a crown."

(From a needlepoint which hung on the living-room wall of my childhood home.)

Unknown:

"All reward is on the other side of risk taken."

Jules Verne:

"Science, my lad, is made up of mistakes, but they are mistakes which are useful to make, because they lead little by little to the truth."

Mathew Walker:

"Absence of evidence is not evidence of absence".

(From: Why We Sleep, Unlocking the Power of Sleep and Dreams)

Christ Episcopal Church Montpelier, Order of Service January 6, 2013:

"Grace us with harmony, good humor, and an active sense of your   presence as we move forward: and all for the love of God. Amen."

The other day I realized that I travel through life on a diet of rationalizations and half-truths, both bursting with functionality. Take for instance my justification for having 10PM snacks. For years I've heard that eating before bedtime is unhealthy, that it produces weight gain. Rationalization #1: I go to sleep much more easily after my snack. Just for the record, I have lost 34 lbs. since 2002.

Rationalization #2: I think of my late-night snack as contributing to, and reflective of, advanced ethical development coupled with diminished olfactory sensitivity. It's a noble act.

When I was eight, I took a baseball bat hit directly to my face. Since then when I look south my nose points southwest. And my olfactory-taste sensitivity is diminished to that of a crow pecking at roadkill. My wife says this analogy fully explains my choice of content for my stir-fries. She has a way with words.

Take the case of our refrigerator. Our family suffers from a totally unjustified sense of food insecurity. On Thursday nights, after grocery shopping, our refrigerator is packed like a Lyons Moving Van. My wife, being a person of Scandinavian moderation, does a full-body shudder as she opens the fridge door.

Rationalizations #3, 4 and 5: I feel ethically compelled to begin emptying the fridge. It's a matter of refrigerator real estate supply and demand, and my wife needs me.

If love is a bright light, composed of a myriad of frequencies, humor must be present as a significant wavelength. At breakfast, with a twinkle in her eye, and a faint smile shared across the table with her mother, my daughter Betsy asks: "So Dad, what did you eat last night for your 10 o'clock snack?"

"A carrot… I ate a carrot."

She glances at her mother.

"Did you eat anything else?"

"Yeah, I had a bowl of cornflakes…with vanilla soymilk. It settles me so I can get to sleep."

She and her mom mirror a wide smile.

"Anything else…Dad?"

"You know that bag of Hershey chocolate Nuggets. You don't have to worry about it anymore. There were only two left in there."

Now their chuckles are getting the better of them.

"Dad, I noticed the pint of Chubby Hubby wasn't in the freezer. You know anything about that?"

"Oh yeah. There was just a little bit left in the bottom."

"Oh my!...Anything else?"

"You know, that leftover Tupperware of stir-fry….I heated it up in the microwave. It was taking up a lot of room in the fridge."

"You'll do anything for Mom, won't you?"

A Carrot

Jesus was a first-century Jewish mystic.

Jesus may have been, and likely was, a charismatic faith healer.

Jesus was turned into a god by people who believed they needed a human divine figure (a Christ, a Messiah).

Much of the Bible (the New Testament) was created to convince people of the divinity of Jesus.

Jesus was murdered by Romans for fear of his political power ("King of the Jews").

Jesus's personal theology and social influence was feared by the existing political-religious establishment.

Jesus was conceived and born like the rest of us.

Jesus died and stayed physically dead.

Fragments of Jesus's teaching have survived.

Jesus's teachings were revolutionary (based on meeting universal human needs).

Jesus took on the role of Messiah knowing he would likely die for taking on this role.

Jesus believed he had a unique mystical communion with a God of Love (Abba).

Jesus was convincing enough to start a multiple-study-group religious sect which was centered on himself and his personal Jewish-based theology as the primary sources of wisdom and life force.

The surviving documents of the teachings of Jesus, as well as the context of the documents, are to be studied, and held to the same standard of validity as any other source. It is likely that much of his teachings, as well as the attitude associated with the teachings, has been omitted and/or distorted by repetition and mistranslation.

It is likely that his teaching of "The Law" can be summarized: Love God with all your heart, soul, and mind, and love your neighbor as yourself.

It is through study and life experience that I have come to believe that Divine Love exists and is the life force on which I acknowledge my spiritual (attitudinal) dependence. I honor that Spirit wherever I am fortunate to detect it. Although far from being the exclusive source, I detect it in the surviving record of Jesus's life and teaching.

After preparing one of my favorite teas and pouring it into my favorite mug, I settle into my favorite chair. As I sip the tea, using my mind's voice, I focus on the following:

I am your Ultimate Interior Audience.

I am Love.

I give you my unconditional acceptance,

my unconditional forgiveness,

my unconditional trust,

my unconditional empathy,

my unconditional humor,

my unconditional presence,

my unconditional appreciation.

And the choice as to how to use them.

It was an emotionally tense Sunday morning at church. Following an earlier all-parish letter, our priest, Kevin, made the announcement of his intention to accept a position at an Episcopal church in South Carolina.

This was a personal loss for me, because I have trusted and admired his integrity, especially his preaching skills. During the past three years I have thanked him repeatedly for his sermons, often commenting on their love content.

After the 10 o'clock service I saw him in the sacristy changing out of his liturgical robe. The stress of the morning was written all over his face.

As I approached him, as if to deliver a comforting word, I said," Kevin, I just want you to feel better, and to be aware that it is a great relief to know we'll be rid of you."

It took a full second before he burst out in uncontrolled laughter.

When did gentle touch become more important than climax?

When did wildflower become more important than lawn?

When did less become more important than more,

And walk become more important than run?

When did adolescent humor become as fun as adolescence?

When did attitude become more important than looks,

And eyes more important than breasts?

When did day become as important as week,

And hour as important as day?

When did gratitude replace entitlement?

Acceptance replace shoulds?

When did partial solution replace completion,

And excellence become more important than perfection?

When did listen become more important than talk?

When did relationship become more important than accomplishment?

When did other become me?

When did I cross over?

AUTHOR'S BIOGRAPHY

Ron Thompson is a Psychologist-Master in private practice in Calais, Vermont. His primary clinical emphasis is to increase empathic understanding and reduce destructive anxiety within individuals, couples, and families. During his twenty-eight years as a clinician, he has worked with people representing a wide variety of mental health challenges, including performance anxiety, depression, generalized anxiety, trauma/abuse, couples and family conflict, interpersonal communication skill deficits, and anxiety secondary to autism.

Drawing on this and coupled with his life-long involvement with classical music, he has developed a psychology of peak performance, Masterful Life-Performance, the principles and practice of which have been applied to a wide range of roles and settings. These include stage drama, music auditions and concerts, public speaking, athletics, preparation for surgery, creative writing, marital intimacy issues, professional and academic test taking, and the performance of daily living.

His book, ON CUE, Managing Anxiety, Inviting Excellence, was judged Outstanding by the 24th Annual Writer's Digest Self-Published Book Awards.

Ron has educational/professional backgrounds in three disciplines: symphonic trumpet performance (Juilliard, National Symphony of Washington D.C.); electrical engineering (University of California Santa Barbara, General Motors Corporation); and counseling psychology (Alfred Adler Graduate School, Minnesota, Vermont Licensed Psychologist-Master).

Pictured with Ron is his wife Maggie, who is a mother, grandmother, homemaker, writing teacher, memoirist, artist, musician, naturalist, Celtic mystic, and bright light in Ron's life.

Ron and Maggie

ACKNOWLEDGEMENTS

Yep, it takes a village, and my writing village is the North Branch Writers' Group, a multitalented bunch of writers who meet for a couple of hours each week under the direction of my wife and life partner, Maggie Thompson, all of whom have contributed, and continue to contribute, to the quality of my writing and the richness of my life. My thanks go out to: Cindy Bogard, Judith Hinds, Sarah Houston, Lyn Kasvinsky, Gail Kilkelly, Justine O'Keefe, Steve Reynes, Cynthia Ross, Terra Trevor, Ben Williams, and Maggie.

A double-thanks (more like quadruple-thanks) goes out to Maggie, who was the content editor for Snippets, and Judith Hinds who did the line editing. My hat is off to Judith for spotting 103 errors. I believe it was Stephen Hawking who said," One of the basic rules of the universe is that nothing is perfect."

Not everyone is fortunate to have a talented artist-photographer in their family. I am.

My daughter Elizabeth has assembled a collection of Snippet photos from family albums and basement cardboard boxes labeled FAMILY PHOTOS, onto which photos she applied her artistic magic. It is a mystery how you do what you do. Thanks, Betsy.

Someone must put it all together in a form that is a bridge to the digital world out there, and Marian Willmott of Willmott Studios, Hinesburg, Vermont has done it, and has been a joy with whom to work. Thanks, Marian.

www.ingramcontent.com/pod-product-compliance
Lightning Source LLC
Chambersburg PA
CBHW061136160726
48006CB00038B/2104